TROUBLED APOLOGIES

AMONG JAPAN, KOREA, AND

THE UNITED STATES

TROUBLED APOLOGIES AMONG JAPAN, KOREA, AND THE UNITED STATES

Alexis Dudden

COLUMBIA UNIVERSITY PRESS   NEW YORK

COLUMBIA UNIVERSITY PRESS

Publishers Since 1893

NEW YORK   CHICHESTER, WEST SUSSEX

Copyright © 2008 Columbia University Press

Library of Congress Cataloging-in-Publication Data

Dudden, Alexis, 1969–
Troubled apologies among Japan, Korea, and the United States / Alexis Dudden.
p. cm.
Includes bibliographical references and index.
ISBN 978-0-231-14176-5 (cloth : alk. paper)—ISBN 978-0-231-51204-6 (e-book)
1. Japan—Relations—Korea (South)   2. Korea (South)—Relations—Japan.   3. United
States—Foreign relations—East Asia.   4. East Asia—Foreign relations—United States.
5. Collective memory—Japan.   6. Collective memory—Korea (South)   I. Title.
DS849.K6D83   2008
303.48′2520519—dc22   2008000514

Columbia University Press books are printed on permanent and durable acid-free paper.
This book is printed on paper with recycled content.
Printed in the United States of America

c   10   9   8   7   6   5   4   3   2   1

References to Internet Web sites (URLs) were accurate at the time of writing. Neither the
author nor Columbia University Press is responsible for URLs that may have expired or
changed since the manuscript was prepared.

For Robert

CONTENTS

ILLUSTRATIONS

PREFACE

China and Japan are the protagonists in most discussions about the unsettled legacies of Northeast Asia's twentieth century, which makes sense. Although we will never know for sure, Japanese soldiers killed between ten million and twenty million Chinese in the nation's attempt to bring China under Japanese control during the 1930s and 1940s. This figure is maddeningly imprecise, yet the toll at either end is so staggering that it remains difficult to approach simple questions of what happened to whom, and how?

Today, the dynamics of history and memory at play in these issues incorporate wide-ranging claims of right and wrong as well as demands for atonement, all of which are subsumed by the local catchall phrase, "history problems." Without challenging China's central place in them, the following pages instead consider how Korea—particularly South Korea—fits in because an interesting pattern runs across Northeast Asia's modern history. As Japan dislodged China as the preeminent power in the region during the first half of the twentieth century, Japanese officials often used policies in China that they had previously tried out in Korea. In other words, and in *no way* a perfect mirror, Japan's takeover and rule of Korea between 1905 and 1945 would serve as a template for Japan's aspirations in China at the time. Notably, the practice continued into the post-1945 world, particularly in terms of Tokyo's policies regarding the nation's collapsed empire. Therefore, looking at Korea and Japan's interactions concerning their shared past may usefully nuance some of China and Japan's more widely known debates.

Moreover, examining Japan's "history problems" with Korea makes clear that any study of these countries' post-1945 relations fails without substantially considering the role of the United States in the matter. Including the United States in this way raises awareness about the limits on writing history, which America has helped sustain in Northeast Asia since the end of the Second World War, leading to related questions about the ongoing nature and meaning of contemporary democracy. Finally, and perhaps most important for most readers, introducing the United States through this lens reveals deep-seated and self-perpetuating boundaries on America's national narratives as well.

ACKNOWLEDGMENTS

Many people and organizations have helped me write this book, which more than anything has convinced me that these problems matter, and that we need to continue to examine why.

Studying apology does nothing if not make you understand that money makes some things real. I would like to thank the Japan Foundation, the Fulbright Program, the American Council of Learned Societies, the Freeman Foundation, the Association of Asian Studies, the American Historical Association, Harvard University's U.S.–Japan Program, Connecticut College, the University of Connecticut, and Columbia University Press for all kinds of support during recent years, which has helped make these ideas into a book.

On top of money, however, studying apology teaches you that without people around you who believe in you and your story it may come to nothing. My family, especially my wonderful husband Robert, numerous friends, teachers, and students have been more than patient and encouraging, yet at the center remains my mother. Unfortunately, she did not get to hold this book in her hands, but more than anyone she kept asking me to write it. I just wish I could show it to her.

TROUBLED APOLOGIES

AMONG JAPAN, KOREA, AND

THE UNITED STATES

CHAPTER ONE

An Island by Any Other Name

The book begins with a tiny group of islands in the sea between Japan and Korea. Migratory birds spend time there, and several rare species of trees, squirrels, and rabbits scratch out an existence on their wind-worn lava cliffs.

History, politics, and law also swirl around these islands now in guises of national security and pride. Japan and Korea both claim them as their own, with Japanese calling them "Takeshima" and Koreans "Dokdo," making them difficult to write about because the book is not trying to pick a winner. Instead, it is trying to describe how these islands—among other things—stand as markers today in the contest to win narrating Northeast Asia's twentieth century. With the important exception of the Korean fishermen killed there in 1948 during U.S. military target practice, these are some of the least bloody lands in the region.[1] That, however, is precisely what makes the arguments around them even more noticeable. Japanese and Koreans are deeply at odds over something that, save for the birds and trees, has grown increasingly empty at the center.

FIGURE I.I Islands in dispute
(From a South Korean government tourist brochure)

Since the end of Japan's colonization of Korea in 1945, Japan and Korea have contested ownership of these islands in closed-door meetings and in widespread public demonstrations, with both sides going to extremes. In 1995, for example, a camera crew from one of South Korea's major television networks camped out on the islands for the entire year, filming each flower as it bloomed and each bird as it arrived to make a detailed point to Korean audiences that the islands were theirs.

The dispute changed key in May 2004, however, when members of an obscure right-wing group in Japan's southwestern Shimane area set sail for the islands in a small motorboat covered with Rising Sun flags to claim them for Japan once and for all. The South Korean government promised full military retaliation should the Japanese men's boat get too close to the rocks. Tokyo loudly proclaimed Japan's sovereign claims while the Japanese Coast Guard guided the men and their patriotically decorated boat home.

The issue of control over these islands has a long and fraught history, and feelings on both sides did not simply melt away once the flag-laden boat returned to Japan. Regional politicians began advocating for national recognition of February 22 as "Takeshima Day," a movement that drew to a head during the first several months of 2005 when the Shimane Assembly organized to vote on the holiday and make it local, if not national, policy. Sponsors of the measure picked the date to commemorate the day in 1905 when Japan incorporated the islands into the nation's now vanished pre-1945 empire, and the Shimane lawmakers wanted to take advantage of the centennial as best they could.[2]

Unlike the previous summer when Tokyo reigned in the extremists and their small boat, the central government made no attempt to stop the regional politicians' movement to declare the islands Japanese. Many wondered whether the ruling party was quietly encouraging the action. To the anger of the South and North Korean governments, as well as millions of Korean citizens, Tokyo described the whole affair as simply a local matter. Japan's ambassador to Seoul, Takano Toshiyuki, made things worse when he told reporters that he did not understand what Koreans were so upset about: the islands were Japanese.

When Shimane assemblymen declared February 22 henceforth "Takeshima Day," anti-Japanese sentiment exploded across South Korea, and Seoul announced that the holiday was "an effective withdrawal of the apologies that Japanese leaders and politicians have made for Japan's past aggressions and imperialist record."[3] Korea's major newspapers and television stations ran weeks of nonstop coverage of the protests and the islands with pundits, politicians, fishermen, and just about anyone else who wanted to talk, explaining over and over that Dokdo was Korean territory and always had been.

In one of the more gruesome acts of protest at the daily gatherings in front of the Japanese Embassy in Seoul, a mother and son pair sliced off their little fingers decrying what they called Japan's resurgent imperialism, and a fifty-three-year-old man claiming to represent families of the victims of Japan's Asia-Pacific War set himself on fire. Seoul city assemblyman Choe Jae-ik traveled to southwestern Japan where Japanese police thwarted his attempt to write a protest in blood on the steps of the Matsue government building. Back in Seoul, Korean police wrestled a pig away from protestors who had named the animal after the then Japanese prime minister Koizumi Junichiro and were preparing to kill it. Korean officials candidly voiced their anger, and South Korea's president at the time, Roh Moo-hyun, even posted a letter on his official Web site demanding that Japan "learn the truth."[4]

Surprisingly enough, all this happened during the first few months of a long and elaborately planned "Year of Friendship" between Japan and South Korea.

What fuels such passion over these rocks? Or, put differently, what is *perceived of* as so important about them that makes people go to such extremes? The fishing areas and natural gas resources around the islands matter to some, of course, but the deeper problem stems largely from the way history troubles the region. The urge to claim them so aggressively now has grown steadily since 1945 with the ways that Japan, Korea, as well as the United States address Japan's colonial era in Korea (1905–1945).

Including the United States in this dynamic may surprise some. Yet, during the second half of the twentieth century, the ways in which each of these countries has dealt with the legacies of the first half of the century in terms of political and legal apologies and apologetic histories has compounded on top of and blended into the earlier era's lived, remembered, and forgotten events. As of today, the process has wound them all into a knot from which none can escape without unraveling the decades of mythmaking that masquerades as national history and has shaped the respective national identities involved.

The obsessive focus on these islands in Japan and Korea ranges from the outrageous to the tragic, a condition mirrored in reverse in the United States by overwhelming ignorance or avoidance. A quick way to grasp the complexity of the problem in American terms comes by knowing that, in the unlikely and highly undesirable event that Japan and South Korea should go to war with each other over these islands, the United States might find itself having to defend the islands for *both* countries because of the separate security and defense treaties it has with each. Although U.S. treaties have attempted to place these islands out of bounds, should actual war break out, the United States might have to align with one of its allies at the cost of the other over dots of land that most Americans never heard of. The incomprehensibility of this state of affairs suggests that determining an owner for the islands is not as easy as it might seem and, more important, might not really solve the problem.

The island dispute is one of many flashpoints between Japan and the Asian nations of its former empire, the most glaring of which is the Yasukuni Shrine in Tokyo to modern-era war dead that houses the souls of regular soldiers as well as convicted war criminals. Today, to the outrage of others in the country as well as countless people throughout Asia and the rest of the world, Japanese politicians visit this shrine to please particular domestic constituencies. Critics wonder how supposedly free, open, and democratic Japan can reconcile state-sponsored worship of men who perpetrated the decimation of tens of millions of lives and entire regions.

With the furor Yasukuni visits cause, as with the island dispute, many scholars and policy makers argue about whether history is really the problem or whether we should allow that Japan and the other governments are simply behaving "rationally" "despite antagonisms" from their shared past, trying to maximize their current interests through manipulation of public sentiment over these issues.[5] If we leave history at the level of how politicians and others deploy reference to things that happened a long time ago for their specific *present* purposes, then, no, history is not the problem per se. Yet this line of reasoning grasps history in terms of what the German thinker Walter Benjamin observed as occurrences in "homogenous empty time," which is an inert space endemic to the modern era in which past events are measured equally to present ones, and whose moments, heroes, and villains are selectively chosen for the present.[6] In other words, in this view, 1905 is just the same as 2005 and can be played with accordingly.

Explaining history in this manner, however, treats it as if it were yet another factor of the present like a trade imbalance or background music. Doing so will not get us any further in understanding why it weighs so heavily on Japanese-Korean relations—among others in the region—let alone grasp what history is. Moreover, it traps those involved in what Harry Harootunian calls "the ruse of history"—a charade that tells a necessary story instead of examining inconvenient truths—which is the "empty time" way that the governments participating in the island standoff use what they call history to justify their respective possession of the islands.[7] The book begins with these islands, therefore, and occasionally returns to them because just a few details of this story shed light on the many histories that have been ignored or rewritten or purely made up to make this currently irreconcilable state of international affairs common sense within national storytelling.

During the spring 2005 standoff, Japanese Prime Minister Koizumi Junichiro responded to Korean hostility over Japan's claims to the islands with the customary, half-hearted pleasantries of "sorrow and remorse for the past" and a need to "face the future together" with Korea. Those unfamiliar with Northeast Asian history and politics may not know what such polite, if formulaic, phrases avoid and what they might have to do with these islands. This is understandable, because the purpose of these terms is to render history an opaque object rather than to open up the messy, contentious, never-ending process that it is. This now-standard apologetic vocabulary has, moreover, been smoothing diplomatic and business relations since 1965, when Tokyo and Seoul signed their Treaty on Basic Relations and began official exchange for the first time since the colonial era ended in 1945. In recent years, these apologetic pleasantries have even fostered an atmosphere conducive to joint military exercises.

Over the years, however, such official niceties have made it all the more difficult for Japanese and Koreans to address the actual content of the so-called past between them, let alone fully appreciate how the past lives and transforms in the present. This includes matters such as the island dispute as well as more internationally known histories like the comfort women system, which involved the commandeering of up to two hundred thousand young women throughout Asia—primarily Korea—to provide sex for Japanese soldiers during the war. The chapters that follow elaborate on some of the problems involved, but for now it is important to understand that various forms of official apologizing for the region's shared history have *themselves* helped generate and spark the unstable present. Although Japanese officials can claim that Japan has apologized for the country's past actions numerous times, victims of that past as well as their supporters have found no dignity in these apologies as far as their particular histories are concerned. Routinely dismissing Korean uproar over the Yasukuni Shrine or the comfort women or possession of the islands, for example, only intensifies the problem.

At first glance in Japan it is difficult—if not impossible—to understand the country's deep modern relationship with Korea. Although many would like to portray Japan's 130 million people as uniform throughout time, since 1945, when the nation's empire disintegrated, Japanese census takers have routinely counted about six hundred thousand people of registered Korean ethnicity among other groups of differing backgrounds in Japan. This may seem a tiny percentage of the population by American standards, but in Japanese terms this means that people of Korean heritage make up more than half of Japan's "other" population. Roughly three-quarters of them descend from the approximately 2 million Koreans who came to Japan forcibly or voluntarily during the colonial era, and, notably, as a group in Japan they now extend into their fifth generation.

The Japanese word *zainichi* translates as "resident foreigner," but it continues to mean "Korean" in practice, marking these people as forever *not* Japanese and denying them citizenship. Unlike the popular Chinatowns in Yokohama, Kobe, or Nagasaki, most Japanese city maps do not specify their Koreatowns, although Osaka residents know, for example, that Ikaino is where the Koreans live. Slums in Japan generally house such a mix of the offspring of the country's former empire, current immigrants, and internal outcastes that no particular name for them would work. Throughout Japan, everyone knows that barbecue restaurants are largely Korean, but with names like "Spring Moon" or "Midnight" they do not disturb the landscape.

Increasingly, in recent years, some *zainichi* have been choosing to live openly with Korean names and embracing their Korean ethnicity, yet—and revealingly—although entertainment stars from Seoul can successfully flood Japanese markets by jetting in from abroad, *zainichi* remains such a nervous category within Japan that its stars such as singer-songwriter Pak Poe are classified under "World Music" regardless that their songs or films or novels are written or performed almost entirely in Japanese and the people involved are born and raised in Japan. Moreover, it remains just as commonplace that the "Tanaka" family next door may appear Japanese until a daughter or son tries to marry into the "Abe" family; then, the investigator hired by the "Abes" discovers that the "Tanakas" are really Korean and are also called the "Chons," or something similar, because voluntary and obligatory concealment is still elemental to *zainichi* existence.

There is nothing in Tokyo like London's Trafalgar Square even to hint at the glory of Japan's once massive empire, which included Korea, unless you count the Yasukuni Shrine, and some do. The largest public display still celebrating Japan's takeover of Korea visible anywhere is a giant mural at New York City's Museum of Natural History that depicts Theodore Roosevelt as host of the 1905 Portsmouth Peace Treaty Conference ending the war between Japan and Russia, which resulted in Korea becoming a victory spoil for Japan. For all practical purposes, unless you know how the early twentieth century operated, you might just think that Tokyo's National Museum naturally has a very good collection of Korean pottery and bronzes.

It is not just in Tokyo, however, where Japanese pretend that Korea and Koreans are, as the cliché so gratingly reminds, "so near and yet so far." Only in 1999 did Hiroshima city officials allow a granite slab dedicated to the approximately fifty thousand Koreans incinerated there on August 6, 1945 *inside* the memorial park. Even still, the poetic phrases adorning the stone do not really explain why the Koreans were there in the first place or how they lived. Instead of big, public monuments, the layered relationship between Japan and Korea more commonly unearths itself on small markers at unannounced sites around the country that quietly record the hundreds of thousands of Koreans who were enslaved in Japan in the 1930s and 1940s in mines, lumber camps, munitions factories, and other industries for the nation's wartime effort.[8] But you should be aware that you might come upon such graves, and, if you do, you have to read Japanese fairly well to decipher the engraving.

By contrast, in Korea, those who have spent even a little time in Seoul know that remembering and forgetting Japan's colonial period is a much more obvious part of the daily terrain. Amid five-star hotels, youth hostels, banks, barbecue restaurants, and night clubs whose staff fluently cater to Japanese tourists and residents of all ages and backgrounds, there are countless structural demonstrations of how the South Korean government has simultaneously reconfigured and effaced its Japanese era self.

A popular landmark in central Seoul, for example, is the old Seodaemun jail, which the city's Parks and Landscape Office suggests should be considered a "holy place" dedicated to the "unyielding spirit of independence" of all Koreans, at home "and abroad."[9] In case the point might be lost, within minutes visitors find themselves in the building's basement where mannequins dressed in Japanese colonial uniforms whip bound and shrieking young Korean girls— also plastic—and appear to commit all sorts of other tortures. A detail you cannot figure out from the costumes or the fearsome Japanese language commands piped in through loudspeakers, however, is that during the colonial era many of the men doing the whipping would have been Korean. In addition to the life-size models, descriptive placards cover the walls to recount Japan's brutal oppression of the Korean people and Korea's general history of resistance to Japanese control. Most are well-known stories, with the added impact of try-them-out-for-yourself solitary confinement cells. Korea's best-known female resistance figure, Yu Kwan-soon, who died a nasty death here after twenty months of torture following her involvement in the mass anti-Japanese riots in 1919, emerges not undeservedly as the sanctuary's Virgin Mary/Joan of Arc icon.

If visitors do not read the signs carefully, though, from the look of things, they might naturally think that the jail would have shut down in 1945 when the U.S. military arrived to liberate Korea from Japan. No signs let the Japanese tourists, the busloads of Korean kids on school trips, or anyone else, for that matter, know that the Koreans employed there by the Japanese instead kept their jobs, never missing a beat working as wardens and torturers in the same jail under the American-backed dictatorships that colored South Korea's political scene for forty years after the Japanese went home. No guide tells you that most of the names scratched on the cell floors and walls date from more recent decades and include numerous South Korean democracy activists from the 1960s and 1970s. Nor can you learn that the last person to be executed there before the prison shut down in the 1980s was the man who assassinated the South Korean dictator Park Chung-hee, who ran the country from 1961 to 1979 with the blessing and assistance of the Americans and Japanese. As is well known but tricky to draw attention to, Park, earlier in his career in the 1930s and 1940s, had learned his leadership skills as a low-ranking officer of Japan's Manchurian Army.

In a different vein, a mile down the road from the prison museum is the picturesque Gyeongbok Palace. It fully reopened in 2002 in time for Korea and Japan's jointly hosted World Cup soccer match after a decade of lavish renovations, including the total destruction of the Japanese colonial governor general's building that had been located there since 1926. If you did not know that Japan had conquered Korea and placed a colossal administration building on that very spot, you would easily miss this detail because a massive, wide-open courtyard has been paved over it. Most of the hundreds of visitors that now come there daily to enjoy changing-of-the-guard displays by actors in stylized seventeenth-century costumes never learn anything about it because its only permanent record appears in small lettering on an obscure sign. Giggling Japanese children posing there today for their school trip photos distract you, furthermore, from knowing either that the American occupation functioned from within this now phantom building between 1945 and 1948 or that it housed Park Chung-hee's cabinet in the 1960s and 1970s.

These and many other purposeful incongruities concerning the twentieth century live themselves out in full view in the center of Seoul and are replicated in countless forms throughout the country. Since the 1965 treaty established relations between Seoul and Tokyo,

FIGURE I.2 Japanese colonial administration building in Seoul, 1994
(Photograph courtesy of the author)

South Korean officials have benefited with their Japanese counterparts from different yet mutually constituting ways of preventing
their nations' shared history of lived events from disturbing the always open present or any anticipated future. In this way, the South
Korean government has worked with Japan according to the apologetic script of "remorse for the past" at the expense of dealing with
the specific content of that past, and, in numerous ways, the United
States has stood powerfully behind (and occasionally within) this
process.

Precisely because of this pattern, however, it was surprising during Japan and Korea's most recent eruption of the island dispute to
hear the South Korean government begin to refrain from its usual
willingness to "face the future" together with Tokyo. Seoul's reluctance hinted, then, that the national narratives holding these stories
in place might finally be coming apart in new and important ways.

In terms of the island controversy, state leaders and supporters in
both Japan and Korea redirect the relevant historical issues in terms
of national security and pride that at once generate broad popular

interest in possessing the islands and foster a reactionary historical consciousness rather than any learning from history. This situation will not bring an end to the standoff, but it has brought into relief deep social anxieties that are blurred by the debate over who owns the islands. In Japan, the controversy combines historical claims to the islands with immediate security fears that highlight pointed and open-ended questions about defining and controlling Japan's contemporary geographical borders. In Korea, the issue of security and borders also figures into the mix, yet the islands reveal more vexing problems with the nation's temporal boundaries and play out more in terms of national pride than security.

MARINE DAY

Since 1945, there have been several spurts of national holiday creation and makeover in Japan. The recent renaming of Greenery Day on April 29 as Showa Day to honor the legacy of wartime Emperor Hirohito's reign (the Showa era, 1926–1989) draws the most attention with critics decrying its obvious nationalist impulse. By contrast, "Marine Day" generates almost no notice. Many have no idea what it is and are just glad for the day off, which, if nothing else, should emphasize the similarity between Japanese people and people in many other parts of the world.

Marine Day first became a national holiday in 1996, and in 2003 the government standardized it to the third Monday of July to coincide with the first day of summer vacation for Japanese schoolchildren. It is admittedly difficult to raise questions about such an inoffensive sounding day. Living in a country that willfully ignores international environmental protocols, I wish the United States had a holiday to "realize our obligations to the ocean" as Japan's Marine Day sponsors ask.[10] From its creation, however, the promoters of this holiday have made it clear that they want the Japanese public to realize the significance of the oceans that surround Japan not simply in terms of their beauty and the resources that lie within them but on a deeper level regarding the potential risks and benefits to national security that these watery domains hold, and this is where the island dispute fits in.

The holiday symbolizes a broadly shifting consciousness about the very nature of Japan's geographic definition and blends into controversies not only with Korea but with China and Russia as well. Many outside the region would be surprised to learn that, since the end of World War II, all these nations have been involved in territorial disputes over various islands and the water around them. Beijing and Tokyo's disagreements over the Diayou/Senkaku Islands in the South China Sea generate the most constant attention because of the multinational companies already involved in procuring and exploring oil in nearby deep sea beds. Moscow's complaint is so entrenched that Russia and Japan are still legally fighting the Second World War over the Kurile/Chishima islands in the Sea of Okhotsk, each refusing to budge until the other gives in over four little islands to the north of Hokkaido.

Admittedly, in a country surrounded by water, Marine Day bemuses some. Responding to a 2002 questionnaire archived on the Web site of the Japan Maritime Public Relations Center, which is the holiday's organizing group, a child in the country's interior asked, "Why isn't there Mountain Day?" A few years ago, during lunch with me on Marine Day in the coastal city of Niigata, one of the city's prominent journalists scoffed at the mention of it: "Ridiculous. Niigata has always been about the ocean. Who needs a holiday?" During recent years, though, the trend has been to see positive meaning for the country in the oceans around Japan, suggesting an about-face from the long-held belief that Japan's island nature equaled national weakness. For some, geography had even *caused* the country's cataclysmic defeat in 1945, yet, in face of such thinking, pundits, politicians, filmmakers, journalists, novelists, and historians have begun looking out again to the seas around Japan to find newly defined meaning for the nation.

Notably, the growing tendency to regard Japan's oceans as a source of national meaning does not necessitate expansionist imaginings, as the late Japanese historian Amino Yoshihiko's work makes clear.[11] Amino introduced his countless Japanese readers to ways of understanding their country's past as difficult and full of opposition and opinion, in large part deriving from its watery borders. In his books, for example, fishermen take on previously undervalued roles in Japanese economic history, and the significance of seaweed, let alone fish, becomes as vital as rice for understanding daily life in samurai times. Primarily, however, the new "island as strength" adherents describe Japan's history and the water around it in futuristic terms, not in terms of the historically lived past. In doing so, they ignore Amino and others' insistence that Japan's geography helps illuminate that the idea of "Japan" is itself an abstraction and something that was created in the past 150 years of the modern era.

Not surprisingly, right-leaning and hard-line right-wing extremist groups promote policy that conceives of Japan on an expanding scale. Although not necessarily organized, these peoples' collective efforts to nationalize Marine Day and to encourage Japanese society to think outward again affirms the mission of the holiday's largest sponsoring group, the remarkably rich and powerfully connected Nippon Foundation. The Nippon Foundation's ostensible origins in 1962 derive from speedboat racing profits, but it should more importantly be understood as a descendant organization of Japan's notorious Mussolini admirer, Sasakawa Ryoichi. Born in 1899, Sasakawa began his career as an Osaka rice market speculator who later amassed a monstrous fortune in the 1930s and 1940s through his exploitative efforts in Manchuria and Mongolia. Known by the nickname "Shadowman," Sasakawa died in 1995, leaving the family foundation to his three sons, who, in addition to sponsoring Marine Day activities such as ocean life seminars, fiestas, and regattas, use the holiday to recruit "volunteers" for a "Maritime Watch" group (*Umimori*). Together with the Japanese Coast Guard, this private force urges citizens to use their cell phones and the Internet to report "suspicious ships, people, and activities" to "protect the security of our seas." All of this is well explained on the organization's elaborately and expensively designed Web site, where you can enroll in their ranks, and, if you like, even order a flag to declare your allegiance.[12]

Significantly, it is not just such eyebrow-raising people who are interested in Marine Day. Japan's widely and internationally ven-

FIGURE I.3 Maritime Watch Flag (Nippon Foundation)

erated journalist, Funabashi Yoichi, shares in the social impetus to expand Japan's spatial sense of self. To commemorate Marine Day in 2004, Funabashi published a feature story called "Japan Needs New Maritime Strategy" that appeared in both the Japanese and English-language *Asahi* newspapers and Web sites.[13] In it, he wrote:

> Although Japan is a small country, with only 370,000 square kilometers of land, its territorial and economic waters make up more than 10 times the land area, totaling 4.47 million square kilometers. Japan is the world's sixth or seventh largest nation in terms of the waters that surround it.

If nothing else, Australia and India might be surprised, but Funabashi's imagined increase of Japan exposes him neither as a megalomaniac imperialist nor a star-crossed dreamer. Instead, this somewhat startling sentence places its author and his newly proportioned Japan squarely within the current mainstream, centrist reasoning and planning for the nation.

For the financial and theoretical supporters of Marine Day, Japan's oceans guarantee the future prowess of an expanded and renewed, solidly bordered nation, as odd as that sounds when water is the defining feature. As a result, therefore, naming the waters around Japan and their contents becomes one with defining national security. Far-flung rocks such as the islands at the center of Japan's dispute with Korea emerge as key markers of the borders that make Japan "Japan." Claiming the islands as "Takeshima," for starters then, would maximize the perceived security that naturally comes with possessing the widest possible spatial limits for the nation.

THE OFFICIALLY VIRTUAL WAR

Although, historically, the Internet is still relatively new, its possibilities as far as social expression and inclusion are concerned already exceed the impact that mass print newspapers first had. Its chaotic nature makes a point of tearing down received truths, and, excitingly for otherwise overlooked history and historians, fosters what Tessa Morris-Suzuki describes as "gladiatorial debates over contentious issues, among them aspects of history that have strong contemporary political resonances."[14] And this is where Japan and Korea's island dispute meets the Internet, with literally millions of Web and blog sites—in English, Korean, Japanese, Chinese, Russian, French, German, Italian, Czech, and Spanish, to name just some of the possibilities—revolving around who owns these rocks.[15]

In a not so subtle effort to control public opinion on the island issue, the Japanese and South Korean governments posted position papers on their foreign ministries' respective Web sites during the recent heated outburst.[16] The official statements diverged in tenor and depth, but both boiled down to drawing lines in the sand: the islands are "ours" not "theirs." If nothing else, the vitriolic approach that the countries' diplomats chose to make public was rather remarkable. Almost as if to entice their "gladiatorial" readers, the governments openly rattled their light sabers in an officially virtual war. Ludicrous, though, remains the school-marmish style of both these sites, as if what the governments of these two democracies say should just do the trick and settle the matter once and for all. This does not work not merely because of the problem of being able to view the opposing explanations simultaneously on your computer screen anywhere you have access to the Web. Rather, it is self-defeating because it reveals how desperately the officials involved are relying on the "empty time/ruse of history" approach even as several more clicks on the Google dial call into question the premise of either or both sides at once.

Significant for our purposes is how the statements on these government Web sites demonstrate the contradictions history causes *even as* both sides claim that history rightly gives them ownership of the islands. At odds is not really which side's argument is truer because the ways in which the governments approach the past yield an incompatible disconnect between space and time, allowing both Japan and Korea to find the truth that each wants. The contradictions matter more for how they elucidate contemporary sources of unease as well as the fictions necessary to sustain the national narratives involved.

As of July 2005, the Web site of Japan's Ministry of Foreign Affairs displayed a position paper in Japanese and English called, "The Issue of Takeshima."[17] The versions read fluidly, notwithstanding the subtle nuances achieved by certain possessive pronouns and adjectives in the vernacular such as "our country's" (*waga kuni no*), which is much like how "the American people" plays out in U.S. political discourse. As ministry bureaucrats would readily confirm, the government's goal is to make Japan's policy transparent, underscoring a desire for English-literate foreigners to read Japan's official statements. There is nothing unusual or new about this. The Japanese government began publishing its major foreign relations aims and accomplishments in both Japanese and English more than a hundred years ago as part of the then newly modernized Meiji government's (1868–1912) effort to describe itself as one among the powerful, imperialist nations of the world at the time.

Korean officials also want to make themselves make sense internationally, and Seoul's Ministry of Foreign Affairs and Trade also publishes English translations of major policies and goals, including its July 2005 document titled "Dokdo: Korean Territory since the Sixth Century."[18] The English-language version is significant here in a slightly different way, however. Ever since Japan annexed Korea in 1910, much of the Korean narrative about this moment has argued that colonization might never have happened had Japan's treachery been better understood: in other words Japanese officials deceived Koreans by using English at the time, which Koreans did not know. The element of Japanese secrecy remains important to Korea's national story, yet it is important to grasp that Japan's use of English at the outset of the twentieth century impressed subsequent Korean governments—as well as Chinese and others in the region—of the need to define their policies outside the Chinese-language sphere, lest they be ignored entirely.

On their Web sites in the summer of 2005, Tokyo and Seoul squared off for a zero-sum match from the outset with Japan declaring:

(1) Based on historical facts and international law, it is apparent that Takeshima is an integral part of Japan's sovereign territory.

(2) The occupation of Takeshima by the Republic of Korea is an illegal occupation undertaken with absolutely no basis whatsoever in international law. Any measures taken with regard to Takeshima by the Republic of Korea based on such an illegal occupation have no legal justification.[19]

And Korea maintained:

The Republic of Korea regrets that Japan is undermining relations between the two nations by challenging Korean sovereignty of Dokdo, an island that has been Korean territory for fifteen hundred years. Korean title to Dokdo is indisputable, borne out by a wide variety of historical and documentary evidences, including documented cases where the Japanese government itself recognized Korean sovereignty of the island. In spite of these facts, Japan is making a groundless territorial claim to this Korean island. Sadly, Japan's claims prompts [sic] Koreans to recall painful memories of brutal Japanese colonial rule, and to ask themselves whether they can cultivate genuine friendship with their island neighbor. As the following paper will demonstrate, Korean sovereignty over Dokdo is truly beyond question or argument. Japan's continued challenge against it—sustained only by disregarding or distorting well-established historical facts—only serve [*sic*] to reinforce our suspicion that the public apologies by Japanese leaders and politicians for Japan's past aggression have been nothing but hollow words and empty gestures.

Both sides' papers then proceed through a list of historical facts to prove their points with Tokyo's main line of argument resting on the country's 1905 incorporation of the islands into Shimane prefecture. Seoul's counter maintains that Korean claims to the islands date from the sixth century, and a lengthy record of diplomatic discussion about them during intervening eras always resulted in Korean control. Thus, regardless of Japan's twentieth-century expansion, the islands have been Korean for much longer, and so they are Korean today.

Right away, the claim to present ownership based on historical justification makes the problem more confusing, not simply because both governments would have you believe one set of statements over the other when both are true: the Japanese government *did* declare the islands part of Shimane prefecture in 1905, and the ancient "History of Three Kingdoms" *does* claim Korean title to the islands in 512. A more fundamental problem arises because both sides display a jarring willingness to ignore how the claims that each makes circumvent themselves in the process of using them as proof, and here is where both governments lead their readers—and themselves—astray.

Tokyo counts on its audience to know next to nothing about the twentieth century nor to have much desire to learn more. Its paper makes no mention that Japan ever colonized Korea nor that this fact might bear on the dispute today.[20] The only hint that Japan's 1905 incorporation of the islands was part of a larger history in progress comes by way of some rather awkwardly defensive statements involving how the islands are Japanese because they have nothing to do with the post-1945 reversion of lands from the nation's collapsed empire.

Conversely, Seoul demands that its audience eagerly follow the contours of a detailed story of the long march of Korean history, in which Japan always acts with treachery concerning Korea, and once Koreans discover what the Japanese are doing to them, they protest without fail on behalf of national interests.

Surrounding all these arguments, of course, was the September 1951 Peace Treaty (known as the San Francisco Treaty), and, revealingly, the two Web sites spin this momentous document in opposing and incompatible directions. The treaty officially ended the Allied state of war against Japan, terminated the American occupation (1945–1952), and, most germane to the island dispute, "restore[ed] full sovereignty of the Japanese people over Japan and its territorial waters."[21]

Moreover, what we think of today as "Japan" had become something radically different in scope by 1945 during Japan's imperialist expansion, spreading the nation's territorial and emotional claims all the way from the western reaches of what was then called Burma to the mid-Pacific Ocean Carolinas in the southeast, halfway up Sakhalin Island in the far north, and covering Manchuria, parts of north China, Korea, and Taiwan.

Immediately following the war, the American government took control of Japanese and South Korean sovereignty, although neither Tokyo nor Seoul concretely mentions this detail on its Web site.[22] By occupying the region, then, the United States involved itself right away in the island controversy and also in Japan and Korea's problems with confronting the lived history of their recent era. In particular, the American drafters of the San Francisco Treaty—and especially John Foster Dulles—exercised enormous power in 1951 when they geographically redefined what "Japan" meant, and the detritus of those decisions exists today in the form of the island disputes Japan has with Korea and also with China and Russia. The treaty effected Japan's loss of the big obvious parts of the Asian mainland as well as the Kuriles, Taiwan, and Jeju, among other islands. At the same time, its authors granted America sole possession of the Bonin islands and Okinawa, which the United States has subsequently "given back," although the sheer magnitude of U.S. military presence on Okinawa today continues to make many there wonder what sovereignty means.

In its 2005 paper, the Japanese government rather disjointedly used the San Francisco Treaty for what it did *not* clarify for the postwar world, stressing that as far as the islands are concerned:

> In the San Francisco Treaty of 1951, it is clearly stated in published United States records that Japan did not include Takeshima in the definition of "Korea," the independence of which was approved and all rights, titles, and rights of claim renounced.[23]

Two things stood out: first, was the negative assertion that because the treaty does not define Takeshima as Korean, it is Japan's, and, second, the deep level assumption that no reader would care that American occupation officials had initially defined the disputed islands as under the jurisdiction of the U.S. occupying army of Korea in a 1946 order known as SCAPIN 677. Only much subsequent wrangling brought about the islands' *lack* of mention in the treaty.[24]

In the devastation that was postwar Japan, the interests of several hundred fishermen notwithstanding, the Japanese general public was preoccupied with survival, not with ownership of some uninhabited rocks that most would not have known about anyway. Yet, in response to the emerging territorial directions that U.S. occupation authorities were taking—delineating the islands as Korean, for example—Japanese Foreign Ministry officials were very interested in who would control these specks of land and began lobbying American officials to maximize what boundaries they could for Japan. In September 1947, ministry officials presented the diplomatic section of General MacArthur's staff with a three-part report expressing Japan's designs on a number of islands including Okinawa, called "Minor Islands Adjacent to Japan Proper: Minor Islands in the Sea of Japan." Korean historian Cheong Sung-hwa has noted that this was the *only* report, throughout the entire occupation, that the Japanese government requested be sent to the State Department in Washington.[25] In this report, Japan claimed sovereignty of the disputed islands based on the 1905 claim in addition to numerous other territorial demands, not the least of which was Okinawa.

Furthermore, in addition to the assumption of the Japanese government's Web site that its audience would prefer a simple understanding of how things happen—the islands are ours because the San Francisco Treaty doesn't say they aren't—it appears to hope that its readers would not be interested in the research that Japanese historian Kajimura Hideki did into the trajectory of that 1947 report. In the 1970s, while doing research in U.S. occupation archives, Kajimura discovered William J. Sebald's July 1950 commentary on a draft of the San Francisco Treaty. On the one hand, this demonstrated that the Foreign Ministry report reached its targeted audience—Sebald was America's chief diplomat responsible for Japan—yet, on the other, it largely confirmed the failure of Japan's efforts to prevent any further diminishing of the country's boundaries at the time.

Among other things in the 1947 report, Japanese urged Americans to understand that it was a mistake to place today's disputed islands within the Korean zone, because "no Korean name exists for the island," and the island is "not shown in the maps made in Korea." In the summer of 1950, William Sebald instructed Washington that the final peace treaty did not need to label the islands Korean as earlier drafts did, because "Takeshima has no Korean name and does not appear ever to have been claimed by Korea."[26] With the Korean War under way, Sebald added, "the islands have been used by U.S. forces during occupation as a bombing range and have possible value as a weather or radar station site."[27]

In other words, although the Japanese Web site does not acknowledge it, the only thing we do know is that, while under American control, the only territorial accomplishment that Japanese officials achieved for maximizing Japan's borders was the San Francisco Treaty's *lack* of mention of the tiny islands at the core of today's aggravation. The treaty lists the richer, inhabited island to the west of today's disputed territory, Ulleungdo, as Korean, for example, yet Japanese officials had spent *much more* energy trying to name this island Japanese, not to mention Okinawa and the Bonin group. Some might see the non-mention of what Japanese call "Takeshima" as a Japanese victory in defining the space of Japan for itself, which might explain why the Japanese government drew attention to this aspect of the treaty in its claim that history justifies its ownership of the islands. The process of how this came about, however, was not quite as matter of fact as the government's argument might have lead readers to believe and is, at best, questionably positive for Japan.

For its part, the South Korean Web site almost encourages the reader to overlook the San Francisco Treaty as a blip on the vast horizon of Korean history while trying to keep its reader focused on earlier times despite the significance this treaty holds over twentieth-century Asian history, world history, and geography. In short, the San Francisco Treaty presents a sticky stumbling block for Seoul in terms of how it might relate to the island dispute today: its signing in 1951 came at the height of the Korean War (1950–1953), and neither South nor North Korea had representatives present, making the lack of Korean participation highlight the question then and now of who controls the Korean peninsula, and, by connection, who controls Korean history.

Because it would have been almost irresponsible, however, not to have responded to Japan's assertion that the San Francisco Treaty grants Japan possession of the islands today, Seoul's Web site addresses Tokyo's negative argument, and you can almost see its authors smiling: "If one follows the Japanese interpretation of the treaty, only three Korean islands would have been returned to Korea (Jeju, Geomundo, and Ulleungdo). Given the fact that there are more than 3,000 Korean islands, such an interpretation is absurd."

Yet, at the same time, South Korea studiously avoids mentioning that Seoul also fell under U.S. occupation (1945–1948) and skips entirely that Korea was embroiled in civil war at the time the San Francisco decisions were made, and that these factors might have mattered to what happened at the time and today. Instead, it justifies control over the islands almost entirely with ancient dynastic maps as well as a plethora of other pre- and early-modern era source materials.

The argument becomes dysfunctional, however, the closer the explanation comes to the present, and it becomes conceptually curious at best when the most difficult yet most germane years of post-Japanese colonization and national division (1945–1953) come into play. One enormous leap of historical faith clear in both the English and Korean texts reads: "Then, after the Second World War, Korea was liberated and regained its entire territory."

Would that this were true. It might have been just as true that the areas of "liberated" Korea that the United States and the former Soviet Union occupied might have been able to establish a unified government that might not have wasted the lives of more than four million Koreans and others in the country's devastating civil war, in addition to shattering many more millions of lives through the country's persistent division. But that would be wishful thinking, not history.

The Korean-language explanation is even more revealing, however, in terms of what is at stake in claiming the islands today. Beginning with the title of the paper and consistent throughout, the South Korean government argues that "Dokdo" is "Korean" using the South Korean name for the country—*Taehan Minguk ui yong'to*—a place that did not exist until 1948, revealing the nation's deeply felt anxieties about claiming Korea's past writ large. Projecting the contemporary name for South Korea onto prior eras enjoins Koreans not just to believe in a past collective identity despite rigid social divisions (including a system of internal slavery) that made this an imaginary non-starter until the late nineteenth century when progressive scholars introduced the idea of a nation and a national body of people. Most powerful, the present claim that South Korean officials make on past eras through the use of "*Taehan*" instead of North Korea's name "*Joseon*" enables Seoul to build consensus that its government is the rightful sovereign of Korea today because of its natural links with Korea's history.

At most, the historical record of the more recent past points to an American decision to avoid the island dispute in print in the San Francisco Treaty. And although some might view this as unfortunate because the treaty might have determined who possessed these islands at the time—as it did for almost all the other territory in Northeast Asia—it actually did not. America's evasion of the matter in 1951 sowed the seeds of the current controversy, yet maintaining that because the document did *not* list the islands and therefore they are Japanese leads us as much in one direction as Korean claims lead in another.

Therefore, Tokyo and Seoul have resolved nothing more than to continue to disagree in incompatible ways, using something called history to do so. By drawing attention to how the U.S. occupation authorities became involved with the problem of possessing the islands, though, they have successfully pointed to the United States as the not so proverbial elephant in the middle of the room, which does not always surface in debates about the island dispute. This is useful because not only would most Americans wonder why they should care about this issue, our top-ranking officials do not even fake understanding it very well. The newly appointed secretary of state Condoleeza Rice arrived in Seoul on her first official tour of the region during the height of the 2005 standoff, equipped to answer a reporter's question about the island controversy with the following statement:

> Now I really believe that these great democracies can deal with issues as they emerge.... It is how strong are your values, how strong are your ideas, how strong is your economy, how much are you able to use the power of your ideas and your influence to change lives around the world.... We and the Japanese friends just talked about a strategic development... and South Korea is an important country in giving development assistance around the world.[28]

One could argue that Rice simply had no idea about the island dispute and that her aides failed her.

A similar line of reasoning might be used to defend William Sebald's instruction to Washington in 1950 in terms of the San Francisco Treaty. Maybe he simply did not know that Koreans also claimed the islands. If this were true, however, Sebald would have been the only person in power in the region ignorant of the situation. In 1948, U.S. Air Force B-52s had bombed and killed scores—if not hundreds—of Korean fishermen, who were gathering seaweed unaware that the islands had been designated off-limits. In 1950, when Sebald made his comment about Korea never having claimed the islands before, some of the dead men's families were in the process of filing reparations claims against the U.S. government, of which Sebald was the chief nonmilitary representative.[29] Likewise, by 2005, given the heightened level of tension surrounding all things Korean following President George W. Bush's 2002 inclusion of North Korea into his infamous "axis of evil," it is alarming to believe that America's highest-ranking diplomat at the time, namely, the secretary of state, knew nothing about a highly charged standoff that she was walking straight into on the ground. But maybe it is true, and Rice in fact did not know.

When President Bush visited Korea in November 2005 during his second state trip to the region, President Roh took the opportunity to urge a resolution to Japan's "historical consciousness problem." As countless newspapers throughout the region reported, Bush leaned in close to the South Korean president and responded, "We hope that the leading nations of Asia will continue to have good relations." Therefore, rather than seeing whole-scale ignorance on Washington's part, it is as easy to understand that American policy has long been avoidance or, as will become clearer, preference for Japan's position at the expense of Korea.

THE EAST SEA

The disputed islands are beautiful, with rocky crags jutting straight up out of deep blue sea. As a tourist, you can go to Dokdo, but you cannot go to Takeshima, as it were, because the South Korean military has stationed several dozen guardsmen there since 1953, limiting safe access to the Korean side. Therefore, although the Japanese government maintains that Korea's occupation is "illegal," neither its right wingers in their flag-covered boat nor other Japanese citizens nor anyone else for that matter can get there from Japan's side without provoking international incidents, unless, of course, you are in the U.S. Navy, which continues to grant you amazing privileges in the air and water of this area.[30]

A several-day trip to the islands from Seoul, done basically, costs about $500. One stays on Ulleungdo and takes a daylong ferry ride to the rocky outcrops in the middle of the sea. This makes it a pretty expensive jaunt for most South Koreans, where the average income is about $20,000. Even with the 2005 uproar, the islands do not compete well with places like Guam or Tokyo for the younger, more disposable income crowd. Foreign visitors are rare, leaving the group riding out on ferries or jetfoils from various ports on South Korea's east coast overwhelmingly South Korean, and overwhelmingly middle-aged and middle-class. In other words, Dokdo's tourists are the mainstay of the so-called Korean miracle.

Others make the trip, of course—especially every South Korean politician who can board a helicopter whenever the issue flares with Japan—and a few summers ago, while waiting for the ferry, I had an interesting exchange with a doctor from the southwestern city of Mok'po. Not more than three sentences into our conversation, he announced that "Korea would go to war with Japan" over these islands. The bravado was as much for me as for his Osh-Kosh–dressed four-year-old son. Yet, it was important that he had no response when I said, "I don't think that the Japanese would fight over them now, yet they might over the name of the ocean around them," which raises the even thornier problem for South Korea and these islands. The sovereignty dispute over the islands bleeds into a broader argument concerning the name of the sea surrounding the rocks. Simply put, although you can only visit the islands from the Korean coast because of how access is controlled, as far as most maps are concerned, you travel through the Sea of Japan to get there. Since 2000, however, the government of South Korea and its supporters have led a multimillion dollar international lobbying effort to change the name to the "East Sea," although, more recently, they have agreed to settle for a joint "Sea of Japan/East Sea" label.

Naming an ocean, of course, has everything to do with geographic borders, yet for South Korea this particular disagreement puts into even starker relief the nation's attempts to assert long temporal boundaries for itself, illuminating Seoul's frustrations over title to Korean history. Like the island controversy, Tokyo and Seoul's foreign ministries use their Web sites to claim the name of this ocean in logic that parallels the island argument.[31] Unlike that debate, however, the Japanese government displays muscular confidence here, featuring a special "Sea of Japan" button that links to an elaborate set of documents to prove that "'Sea of Japan' is the mono-name of the area, recognized internationally. Government of Japan takes this position since past and is determined to argue against the assertion without any ground [*sic*]."[32] Again, the South Korean foreign ministry invokes what it calls history and argues that older records name the sea Korean. Calling this body of water by Japan's preferred name would, Seoul insists, be yet another extension of Japan's nineteenth- and twentieth-century imperialism, the era during which it claims the Sea of Japan name gained global currency. This claim immediately loses ground, however, because the Japanese government has proudly countered with a mind-bogglingly detailed study of 1,435 maps catalogued at the U.S. Library of Congress (August 2005), 407 maps at the Bibliothèque Nationale de France (March 2004), and more than 200 maps at the British Library and Cambridge University (September 2003) showing that, no, in fact the gradual cartographic shift toward using the name Sea of Japan began in the late sixteenth and early seventeenth centuries before Japan could, as Tokyo phrases, "exert international influence."

Seoul's biggest challenge stems less, however, from the always tenuous "blame Japan" game than from its internal attempts to use history to justify why this body of water should be recognized today as the East Sea. There are sixth- and seventh-century maps that use this name, yet most of the maps that Seoul and Tokyo use as evidence and display as proof for their claims date from more recent times (largely the seventeenth century on). On these maps, whenever the sea in question is labeled as "Korean," almost invariably the name is the Joseon Sea or the Korean Sea, which defines Seoul's current problem. Because the body of water never appeared on Korean or foreign maps as the Republic of Korea Sea, Seoul cannot find in history a name that would align the water with its current self, so it must go out of its way to dredge up the archaic East Sea name to avoid North Korea's choice—the Joseon East Sea—because this *more* historically defensible name would incorporate the word for Korea that Pyongyang uses for the nation today. South Korea's effort to give this sea a Korean name—one that would atmospherically bolster its efforts to claim sovereignty over the disputed islands that lie within it—defeats itself by so frantically running away from the country's own twentieth century.

Exhibits at the government-run, Samsung corporation–backed Dokdo Museum on the neighboring Ulleungdo island confuse the problem in even more unresolved ways, making their note of unease a good place to move on to the next chapter. The museum opened in 1997, with the mission of countering Japan's "absurd insistence" about possessing the disputed islands. As the nation's leading conglomerate—and not the only one whose Japanese colonial-era origins involve a privileged young Korean man educated in Japan—Samsung's stated purpose in donating the architecturally savvy building stems from its commitment to "our country."[33] Seeing me smile at the Samsung sign at the entrance to the museum, an astute Korean journalist with whom I visited the spot in 2004 smiled in return, and said, "Samsung is so global it *has* to be at the forefront of Korean patriotism, so Koreans keep buying their products and working for them without following where their money or their jobs go."

Following up on its collective thematics of history, according to Samsung the islands have been "ours since 512 AD." The word "ours" resonates vividly here. Dozens of Dokdo tourists and Ulleungdo residents sing the popular ballad "Dokdo Is Our Land" on the ferry out to the island.[34] More broadly, though, it features prominently into all flavors of South and North Korean unification discourse, allowing Koreans to be Korean and overcome the twentieth century with a simple pronoun.[35] A banner hanging in one of the exhibition halls over various historical maps confuses everything, however, by avoiding any mention of "our" sea and instead declaring that, "The East Sea is a directional concept, and the Joseon/Korean Sea is the proper noun." Only about five thousand people make it out to the disputed islands annually, yet more than one hundred thousand visitors come to this museum on Ulleungdo. Explanations of how history works for Korea against Japan here invigorates pride in being Korean, while obscure injunctions such as this one only further massage the fundamental problem in being "Korean" right now—in ways unlikely to disturb South Korea's or Samsung's investments north of the border—suggesting that there are much larger disputes ahead in naming "Korea" and its history.

In November 2006, on the sidelines of the Asia-Pacific Economic Cooperation (APEC) summit meeting in Hanoi, when South Korean president Roh Moo-hyun first met with Japan's then recently instated prime minister Abe Shinzo, the former suggested ending Korea and Japan's antagonism by calling the ocean, "the 'Sea of Peace,' or the 'Sea of Friendship,' or even the 'Sea of Understanding' as a new launching point for Korean-Japanese dialogue."[36] Apparently Abe did not respond, yet once the comment surfaced back in Seoul, Roh's own party as well as the opposition jumped on him for being inconsiderate of Korean people's feelings.

In a different vein, several years earlier during the summer of 2002, a middle-aged Japanese woman living in suburban Tokyo wrote a letter to the editor of the *Asahi* newspaper saying that she thought the ocean should be called the "Blue Sea."[37] She wanted to move beyond the ingrained positions and draw attention to the water's beauty as well as the environmental challenges both countries face with its future. To many, such a suggestion might seem naïve or even absurd. But after more than half a century of living within the "ruse of history," how could her idea be any sillier than what the governments involved offer? The "empty time" approach continues to make the entwined histories devoid of their substance, which ultimately cannot work because history does not work that way.

Official and semi-official voices in Japan, South Korea, and the United States each reveal a distinct essence in narrating their nations' pasts for present purposes. For some, the three chapters that follow may ask more questions than they answer, yet their aim is to focus attention on a variety of inner-connected histories that refuse to go away no matter how they are spun.

CHAPTER TWO

Apologies All Around

What is so important about apologies anyway? Until about twenty years ago, the kind of international political apology that draws such attention nowadays was quite rare. One of the first apologies in Japan's modern history took place in 1872 after an American working for Japan's Ministry of Colonial Affairs in Hokkaido got drunk and demolished the house he was living in, then injured two Japanese men working for him, and finally shot five hunting dogs that belonged to the local native Ainu chief. The Japanese government feared protests from the Ainu whom they were beginning to assimilate as Japanese, and, through its pressure, American officials ordered Major A. G. Warfield to write an apology for his actions:

> To the Japanese Government: Whereas on the morning of the 29th October I was under the influence of whiskey to such a degree that I was unconscious of what I was doing . . . I hereby apologize both to Numera, Nangi, and the Japanese government for what I have done.[1]

Warfield apologized as an individual, not as the U.S. government, and yet his words calmed things down as far as local relations were concerned.

Throughout the twentieth century and around the world there were numerous apologies, mainly formal state to state ones for events such as wars and shipping accidents, with most involving some sort of indemnity. All were carefully scripted according to prevailing international laws, and most were well catalogued in government document books. Things began to change, however, with the post–World War II development of war crimes tribunals and the judgment of one nation over another. The big shift, though, came two decades ago when Richard von Weizsäcker, president of what was still then West Germany, publicly said he was sorry for his nation's history, fundamentally transforming everything about apology and touching off an international apology boom.

On May 8, 1985, during his speech commemorating Germany's fortieth anniversary of defeat, Weizsäcker apologized for the country's former Nazi regime, which, for many, trumped even Willy Brandt's famous 1970 wordless collapse in front of the monument to the Warsaw Ghetto uprising. Ever since Weizsäcker's speech, Germany has been regarded as the world's apologetic model in terms of addressing bad history. Whether or not the standard is perfect, it took hold, and an apology movement took off around the world, making heads of state the mouthpieces of new official histories. In many cases, the statements leaders issued reversed long-standing practices of purposeful forgetting, or, as the social critic Norma Field so eloquently observed, "What had been official blasphemy seemed to become, overnight, commonsense."[2]

In large part, civic groups acting with and on behalf of victims of state-sponsored violence rallied together to bring about these apologies, and victims, activists, and their sympathizers came to regard them as a primary goal. When government officials apologized for historical horrors like slavery, for example, many counted it as an achievement, sustaining an ongoing commitment for more. At the same time, however, state leaders increasingly co-opted apology to make national apologizing work to strengthen the state. In other words, although many would continue to frame apology solely in terms of a victory for the state's victims, the state's protagonists simultaneously managed to make apologizing a means with which the state could continue with business as usual.

Essentially, throughout the 1990s and into the beginning of this century, leaders learned to address wrongs that the international community perceived as abnormal to its collective sense of self. The extent to which participants engaged in apology politics depended on local aspirations to power in the international system. Simply put, apologizing came to define those issuing them as "normal" or "good-standing" members of the global community.

Japan's leaders were no different. During the 1990s, officials began debating Japan's interests as a "normal" state ("noma-ru" in Japanese), which, save for the few remaining Communists, almost all would now define as requiring a proactive military less dependent on the United States and a permanent UN Security Council seat. Most noticeably in the years surrounding the 1995 fiftieth anniversary of the end of the war and the turn of the century, there appeared at times to be a constant stream of apologies for Japan's attempt to control Asia during the first half of the twentieth century. In other words, therefore, official apologies became deeply entwined with the pursuit of national interests, and the country's conservative ruling party, in particular, veered toward the practice. Leaders maintained that it was pragmatic for Japan to apologize for something called "the past" because doing so would affirm the nation's current and future ties with its Asian neighbors.[3] Though largely overlooked, since 1992 Japan has issued at least twenty official apologies for the nation's twentieth-century record.

Despite the official pronouncements of "remorse," however, Japan remains embroiled in what are known throughout the region as the "history problems," which are hostage almost entirely now to political policy, meaning that they are no longer about history (if they ever were). In short, Japan's way of apologizing only perpetuated a disastrous policy failure since so many found Japan's words so hollow.

Japan's apology failure—not its failure to apologize—stems from the problem that, although quite a few Japanese officials have made

statements of "remorse" and "heartfelt apology," they and Japanese
society in general have far to go in making the substance of the nation's twentieth century elemental to modern Japanese history in
the same way that Native American genocide and African slavery
in this country, for example, must *continue* to be understood in
shaping the history of the United States. For starters, Japan's
multimillion-dollar denial industry would have far less traction in
Japan today were a majority of Japanese convinced that the subject
matter of its politicians' apologies—the human cost and structural
legacies of Japan's empire and total war—were of crucial importance
to contemporary Japanese social and ethical concern.

Put differently, how could a survivor of one of Japan's slave labor
camps believe the Japanese government's words when a not insig-
nificant number of its democratically elected politicians and highly
paid pundits routinely make speeches and publish wildly popular
books denigrating the survivors' claims or look soberly into TV
cameras and say they are making it all up? If anything, such voices
are only amplifying in Japan these days.

Although often thought differently, the government of Japan did
not dramatically lag behind Germany with its initial stabs at apology. In 1965, for example, Japanese diplomats made public statements in Seoul about the need to "reflect" on the countries' "shared
history."[4] In 1972, Japanese officials issued similar pronouncements
when establishing relations with Beijing, and, in 1984, Japan's wartime emperor Hirohito himself followed the nation's apologetic formula by expressing his "regret" to South Korea's visiting president
Chun Doo-hwan for the "unfortunate period" that the countries
had in common.[5] Admittedly, these expressions were lukewarm at
best, but were they really more inherently ambiguous than the
German leader's silent prayer?[6]

Without question, however, Japanese society has not gone nearly
as far as Germany's in terms of incorporating the state's history of
violence into school education, among other things. This became
wildly clear during the 1990s, when, in the wake of Emperor Hirohito's 1989 death, within Japan it suddenly seemed that everything

about the war and empire was all being said at once, and, for many, for the first time. Unlike Germany where, since the 1960s, public education has at least made most people aware of stories of death camps and pogroms and collapsed expansionist nightmares, in Japan news of wartime atrocities that Japanese committed seemed to appear out of nowhere for most, raising new questions about the meaning of history itself.[7] Furthermore, the Asian places of Japan's former empire were themselves experiencing budding democratization movements at the time. As a result, from Seoul to Jakarta, voices that had long been silenced by their own leaders in the name of post-1945 national interests—from former comfort women to former conscripted soldiers and former slave laborers—suddenly found audiences receptive to their stories at home as well as abroad.

In his 1999 essay, "Air War and Literature," the extraordinary writer W. G. Sebald confronted postwar German literature's avoidance of the Allied (particularly British) obliteration of Germany's cities (particularly Dresden) and their inhabitants.[8] "The destruction, on a scale without historical precedent," wrote Sebald, "entered the annals of the nation, as it set about rebuilding itself, only in the form of vague generalizations."[9] In marked contrast to Germany's apologists who use the bombings of Dresden and Hamburg and elsewhere to divert attention away from the nation's homegrown genocides, however, Sebald explained the interconnection of these histories in terms of the national psyche as follows:

As far as I know, the question of whether and how (the Allied campaign) could be strategically or morally justified was never the subject of open debate in Germany after 1945, no doubt mainly because a nation which had murdered and worked to death millions of people in its camps could hardly call on the victorious powers to explain the military and political logic that dictated the destruction of the German cities.[10]

For Sebald, the problem of German authors dancing around this destruction was too large to ignore: the empty center they created "served primarily to sanitize or eliminate a kind of knowledge incompatible with normality...and allowed [West German society] to recognize the fact of its own rise from total degradation while disengaging entirely from its stock of emotions, if not actually chalking up as another item to its credit its success in overcoming all tribulations without showing any sign of weakness."[11]

In many ways, the opposite conditions were true for Japan, and their impact cannot be underestimated. During most of the decades following the war, Japanese writers and social critics openly debated the meaning for Japan of the Allied (particularly American) destruction of Japanese cities (particularly Hiroshima).[12] At the same time, however, a social taboo suppressed discussion and education about atrocities that Japanese soldiers and colonists committed abroad in the emperor's name. Put differently and in the broadest strokes, after a period of coming to terms with survival that lasted until the early to mid-1950s, from then on through the early 1990s Germans deliberated their nation's attempted annihilation of the Jews but not the firebombing of Dresden, whereas Japanese ruminated on the wastelands of Hiroshima and Tokyo at the cost of confronting Japan's devastation of large parts and populations of Asia.

This collective impasse in Japan stems largely from what is known as the "Chrysanthemum Taboo" for its symbolism of the imperial family. In simplest terms, this taboo is a social prohibition against publicly raising the question of the emperor's involvement in the war, as well as all the histories that hang in *that* history's balance. With Hirohito's 1989 death, the possibility of this spell vanishing found new life and in no small way triggered the avalanche of materials concerning the first half of the twentieth century that appeared in bookstores, newsstands, art museums, city halls, schools, movie theaters, and TV shows throughout the country during the 1990s.

Between 1900 and 1945, when millions of Japanese expanded and defended their nation's empire in the name of Emperors Meiji, Taisho, and Hirohito, Japanese law defined the emperor as follows:

The Emperor is Heaven-descended, divine and sacred; he is pre-eminent above all his subjects. He must be reverenced and is inviolable. He has indeed to pay due respect to the law, but the law has no power to hold Him accountable to it. Not only shall there be no irreverence for the Emperor's person, but also shall he neither be made the topic of derogatory comment nor one of discussion.[13]

The emperor was supposed to be forever clean regardless of what Japanese people were doing in his name, and ultimately it would be up to him to judge his subjects' actions dirty should he wish.

Only in January 1946 did the terms of the emperor's existence change. In his customary New Year's Day greeting, Hirohito announced that he was not a god: "The ties between us and our people have always stood upon mutual trust and affection. They do not depend upon mere legends and myths. They are not predicated on the false conception that the Emperor is divine."[14] He did not have too much farther to fall, however. By the end of the month, the American occupation authorities controlling him and Japan made it clear that the emperor was not a war criminal. Rather, he was a victim of circumstance, which was how the Japanese people in general would eventually be described in the preponderance of national storytelling that took its cue from this decision.

In other words, even though at the time many in Japan and around the world were aware that millions of Japanese had committed all kinds of violence against millions and millions more abroad and at home to honor Hirohito's rule, he would not be responsible for any of it. In a telegram back to Washington from Tokyo, General MacArthur determined that evidence to the contrary was not "specific . . . with regard to [Hirohito's] exact activities" and that "his connection with affairs of state up to the time of the end of the war was largely ministerial and automatically responsive to the advice of his councilors."[15] Thanks to American intervention, therefore, Hirohito, for the most part, lived comfortably for the next four decades in Tokyo's imperial palace in his new role as a nature loving biologist, forcefully forgetting his empire's war for himself and his country.[16]

Of course, many Japanese would not change overnight the beliefs they once held about the emperor or at least about his place in Japanese society.[17] Moreover, many of those in Japan who benefited from not delving into Japan's record of violence fed the "Chrysanthemum Taboo" by publicly humiliating or threatening those who touched on the historical substance of Japan's empire and war between 1900 and 1945. The chief sustainers of the taboo included pardoned war criminals who had returned to parliament, big businessmen whose coal mines and rubber plantations had thrived on Asian and Allied POW slave labor, as well as countless average soldiers who did not want to confront or be confronted with the atrocities they had committed abroad in their emperor's name.[18] The victims of the hex, on the other hand, included a wide variety of historians, journalists, schoolteachers, writers, artists, and filmmakers, among others, some of whom lost their jobs or had their careers marginalized simply for urging others to take a look at what had happened earlier in the century.

One reason the "Chrysanthemum Taboo" functioned so easily right away was that, although Hirohito disavowed imperial divinity, he did not publicly challenge the earlier law that forbade "irreverence," "derogatory comment," or "discussion" about him. This gave enormous flexibility to those intent on sustaining the myth of his greatness to justify the empire built and fought over in his name. In the decades following Japan's defeat, those defining modern Japan's national story saw to it that anyone engaging history in any way that suggested disdain for the emperor or the system he upheld would identify that person as questionably "Japanese." Foreigners were one thing and their work could be ignored or ridiculed. Yet, in a society that continues to pride itself on homogeneity, for decades Japan's postwar democratic leaders tried to estrange Japanese who tried to unravel the nation's most immediate past from within.

The most famous of Japan's voices against this powerful postwar storm was the delightful yet far from radical historian Ienaga Saburo. Ienaga was a high school teacher in northern Japan during the war, and he often said later that his greatest personal shame was failing to resist teaching the required wartime propaganda, which included the myth of fighting for a divine Japan. As a result, Ienaga felt responsible for sending some of his students off to war, which informed his determination to write about what happened during the war to educate future Japanese in the nature of actual, not mythical, fighting. His attempt in the early 1950s to publish a Japanese school textbook that mentioned various notorious histories such as the Nanjing Massacre caused Japan's Ministry of Education to demand more than two hundred cuts and changes. He refused on the grounds of postwar Japan's constitutionally and democratically enshrined principle of freedom of speech. And, in 1965, Ienaga began a life-defining series of lawsuits against the Japanese government that involved hundreds of lawyers and thousands of supporters from Japan and throughout the world. He even received a 2001 Nobel Peace Prize nomination for his efforts. Like his lawsuits, however, which saw moments of hope during the 1990s but never fully achieved their aims, the nomination failed. Ienaga died in 2002 at the age of eighty-nine.

During the 1990s apology boom, whenever Japanese officials commented on Japan's modern history, their statements were viewed—as sociologist Jeffrey Olick observed in a related vein—"*in reference to*" well-known German pronouncements, not simply in terms of their own content.[19] As such, they never quite measured up.

One consequence of the overwhelming emphasis on Japan's shortcomings compared to Germany's achievements was to garner the resolve of those in Japan who never favored the idea that Japan should apologize in the first place. The unrelenting "Why can't Japan be more like Germany?" charge furthermore frustrated even those supportive of apology, and, as a result, as of today the anti-apology apologists for Japan's histories of violence have accrued increasing common sense to their contention that Japan did not do anything worse than anyone else. The core understanding of those seeking atonement may again be lost. The histories that will *always* need to be thought about are once again out of the schoolbooks or on the verge of erasure.

In November 2004, for example, public officials such as the education minister Nakayama Nariaki had this to say about the diminishing number of references to wartime atrocities in the nation's texts: "That's good. We shouldn't focus so much on the negative."[20] More widely disseminated affirmations of this trend followed Prime

Minister Abe's March 2007 denial that the thousands of women and girls involved in Japan's infamous comfort women system had been "coerced." His party's policy chief, Nakagawa Shoichi, for one, seemed to presume that the public had not watched television or read newspapers during the 1990s, when survivors appeared routinely to recount their lived nightmares and unhesitatingly told reporters, "There's currently no evidence that permits us to declare the military, the strongest expression of state authority, took women away and forced them to do things against their will."[21]

In starkest relief, such sentiment reveals a conviction that the non-Japanese human cost of modern Japan's wealth and power is both irrelevant and destructive to a collective sense of being Japanese. In December 2006, in the face of a small yet articulate and poignant protest, the Japanese government achieved what was for some the long-desired goal of revising the 1947 education law, one of the pillars of postwar reform. Once again, a primary aim of public education will be to instill a "love of country" in young Japanese, which is admittedly more difficult to do if you study things like massacres and slave camps in too much detail.[22]

Now, more than sixty years after the end of the war, the remaining survivors of wartime atrocities continue to want their stories heard and measured as significant to modern Japanese history, and yet they are more and more openly derided as only "in it for the money." Those sympathetic to the victims and to dispelling the "Chrysanthemum Taboo" which discredits them and their histories are again on the defensive, searching for more evidence to prove the already horrible even worse.

A BRIEF HISTORY OF REMORSE

As mentioned before, toward the end of the twentieth century the Japanese government made a number of apologies concerning the first half of the century, the most elaborate of which was Prime Minister Murayama Tomiichi's 1995 statement on the fiftieth anniversary of Japan's defeat:

Our country, through its colonial rule and aggression, caused tremendous damage and suffering to the people of many countries, particularly to those of Asian nations. In the hope that no such mistake be made in the future, I regard, in a spirit of humility, these irrefutable facts of history, and express here once again my feelings of deep remorse and state my heartfelt apology.[23]

Regardless of some rather brazen attempts to overturn this statement and other similar apologies, groups as central to power as Japan's foreign ministry as well as Prime Minister Fukuda Yasuo state that these words continue to define the nation's official view of Japan's twentieth-century history in Asia.

In its wake, Japanese politicians of all parties converged on this so-called Murayama declaration, with holdouts on the Far Right getting vastly more press than their counterparts on the Left.[24] Yet, although it became commonplace for Japanese officials to talk about "sorrow" and "remorse" for an unnamed "past," it became *as* common for victims of that "past" and their supporters to dismiss these statements as lacking in substantive meaning. This opinion was not necessarily misplaced, but it trapped those who agreed. Well-organized networks supported the resolve of many of those demanding an apology, and in doing so they created the problem of who would decide when an apology was ever "real." For many victims of Japan's state-sponsored violence, no apology would ever suffice. Some, for example, asked for a direct, personal apology from the emperor and others wanted Japan's parliament to enact a law condemning its own past, neither of which would appear to be looming on the horizon.

Important always to bear in mind, unless the victim of any wrongdoing accepts the apology at hand, it will remain hollow, regardless of how often someone repeats it. Imagine an English-speaking tourist in the middle of a place where no one speaks English. No matter how many times the tourist asks the same question and no matter how loudly he or she repeats it, there may be no communication at all, despite how friendly or unfriendly everyone involved is. In terms of Japan's official apologies during the 1990s, this pattern played out repeatedly between the government of Japan and various victims' groups, further fueling the belief that Japan's apologies would never measure up to Germany's and fanning the fires of those against apologizing for anything anyway.

On this point, Japan's post-1945 relations with Korea reveal that the government of Japan has long been concerned with not letting some of the nation's more troublesome histories undermine its present or future. In other words, the apology and history problems did not just spring out of nowhere in the 1990s when the apology movement gained momentum worldwide. To be sure, people started to pay more attention at the time for reasons ranging from the increasing lack of living survivors to the wild ride of ever globalizing national economies in the 1990s. This particular history demonstrates, however, some important features of Japan's apologetic techniques with Korea that have been hidden in the recent spate of apologies all around.

In June 1965, after thirteen years of protracted negotiations, Japanese and South Korean diplomats established relations that many describe as "normalizing" or as "coming to terms with the past." This moment thus officially began Japan's decolonization process with Korea. It is important to understand that the 1965 agreement inaugurated—not recommenced—South Korea and Japan's relations as independent states. Before Japan's 1910 colonization of Korea, Tokyo had relations with the entire peninsula, which it then usurped by annexing the country into the Japanese empire. In August 1945, the creation of American and Soviet occupation zones carved Korea in two, meaning that, in essence, there were no official relations between occupied Japan and occupied South or North Korea, only relations between the various occupation authorities involved, and even those were quite confusing at best.[25] In 1948, South and North Korea respectively came into existence, a condition made further real after the Korean War by the terms of the 1953 armistice between Pyongyang and Washington, which, as far as North Korea was concerned, gave it greater legitimacy than the South, which had to rely on the Americans' signature to end the fighting.[26] Therefore, in 1965, South Korea's decision to begin relations with the country's former overlord without the North's participation generated additional tensions between Seoul and Pyongyang, not in the least because the UN-sanctioned 1965 Treaty on Basic Relations Between Japan and the Republic of Korea (South Korea) declared South Korea the sole legitimate government of the peninsula in terms of international conventions and protocols at the time.[27]

Although the 1965 treaty established Tokyo and Seoul's relations, Washington was far from absent in the process. As American interests in Vietnam grew in the early 1960s, Washington wanted to free up some of the funds it was spending on development and military aid in South Korea to use to defend its latest bulwark against communism, and it wanted to transfer some of the Korea burden to Tokyo.[28] America's famous ambassador to Japan, Edwin O. Reischauer, had watched the years of failed negotiations between Japan and South Korea and strongly emphasized to Tokyo the need to formally address Korean resentment over colonization for progress to be made. Despite Tokyo's reluctance to get things going, Reischauer held firm to his position that Japan should make some sort of statement about the colonial era, and, in the months leading up to normalization, Japanese officials made statements revealing the critical role the U.S. played in the development of Japan's apology politics with South Korea.[29]

Of subtle yet monumental importance, Reischauer, during this time, offered the phrase "unhappy history" to describe the recent past of Japanese-Korean relations. In pragmatic terms, it was pure genius to freeze the past into an indeterminate time period for which no one was to blame. This, however, is precisely what continues to anger those seeking recognition of specific histories, because, ever since then, Japanese and South Korean diplomats and politicians have repeatedly "regretfully" dissolved "the past" into equally vague phrases concerning the nations' future together. This vocabulary took root and emerged as the most powerful apologetic technique in play, and Japanese leaders finally solidified it in writing during the 1990s when similar terms flourished worldwide.

In September 1964, Reischauer wrote a memo to Secretary of State Dean Rusk acknowledging that "clear Japanese apology for their colonial oppression of Korea in past" was difficult, because "Japanese officials and public simply do not feel they owe any apology to Koreans."[30]

In November, he sent a telegram to Rusk to report on his breakfast meeting with Foreign Minister Shiina Etsusaburo during which he urged Japan to make "some sort of apology to Koreans for colonial past." When Shiina's secretary suggested that the foreign minister's upcoming visit to Korea would come "as close to expression of apology as was feasible," Reischauer urged that "some sort of forward-looking statement about turning backs on past unhappy history... might assuage Koreans' feelings without irritating Japanese public."[31]

Early the following winter, in February 1965, Shiina visited Seoul for several days. Socialists in Japan protested the ruling party's decision to launch relations with Seoul at the expense of Pyongyang by organizing a no-confidence vote in the Diet, and students in both countries held demonstrations to protest North Korea's exclusion from the settlement. Japanese Prime Minister Sato Eisaku and South Korean President Park Chung-hee, however, were determined to make Shiina's visit a success at all costs. When Japan's foreign minister arrived at Seoul's Kimpo airport, he immediately declared Japan's "regret" for "the unfortunate period" the countries shared.[32]

Shiina told waiting reporters, "I believe we should reflect deeply on the truly regrettable circumstances of the unfortunate period in the midst of our nations' long history. . . . It is in these hopes that we establish future-facing permanent and friendly relations on which we can build a new respectful and prosperous history." The countries had not yet established diplomatic relations, and this moment marked the first Japanese official public statement in Korea—South or North—about the colonial era. *Asahi* newspaper special correspondent, Imazu Hiroshi, noted Shiina's statement as highly significant, and he conveyed his own hopes for improvement.[33] At the same time, James C. Thomson Jr., of Lyndon B. Johnson's National Security Council Staff, remarked that "Shiina came as close as a Japanese can to apologizing for Japan's sins, and everyone—including State—is thoroughly pleased."[34]

The rigidity of such a formulation is clear, however. Until recently, not only did it forestall delving into the histories in question, the governments' reliance on these words disgraced survivors of any number of violent events by saying, in effect, "that was then, this is now, you don't matter to our future, and therefore your past must be swallowed for the benefit of our present." Tokyo and Seoul have not necessarily denied the past, but victims were long left with no option for protest. Even during the more open 1990s, survivors found themselves often doing no better than running along a spinning wheel of the state's creation in courts that ultimately would remain indifferent to their claims.[35]

Although Reischauer's involvement reveals American pressure on the process, Japanese and South Korean officials subsequently chose to maneuver within the boundaries of this formula and make it their own. On October 8, 1998, three decades after Shiina's statements at Kimpo airport, and after three decades of Japanese and South Korean officials using these terms, Japanese Prime Minister Obuchi Keizo issued Japan's first written declaration about the "unfortunate past" together with South Korean President Kim Daejung. The declaration is largely a continuation of the same theme, combining long-standing words of "remorse" and "heartfelt apology" with the 1995 Murayama statement.[36] Self-described pragmatists congratulated themselves and heralded it as a groundbreaking statement that would usher in an era of "new partnership."

The declaration perpetuated other problems, however, immediately suggesting that simply putting the usual phrases into writing might not produce new solutions to the histories at hand. In fact, the written version might even generate more complications. For starters, the "joint declaration" once again referred to the "unfortunate past" that caused the history troubles in the first place and yet inscribed it as "a certain period in the past," rendering it even more imprecise. Deciding still to avoid determining *when* this history took place, of course, has only continued to make it possible to defer the problem of who might take responsibility for it.

Second, and related to South Korea's own conundrum of how to project itself onto any Korean history that predates the nation's birth in 1948, the 1998 statement acknowledged that "Japan caused . . . tremendous suffering and damage to the people of the Republic of Korea through its colonial rule." The problem is that there was no Republic of Korea during the time of Japan's colonial rule, which points to how the official way of referring to the past between Japan and Korea has served until very recently to define South Korea as the rightful government on the Korean peninsula.[37] In fact, until September 2002, when Japanese Prime Minister Koizumi traveled to Pyongyang for Japan's first head of state meeting ever with North Korea, all of Japan's official proclamations about history referred only to South Korea—*Nikkan*/日韓—quietly carving South Korea's privileged position into stone. None of these issues existed during the "certain period in the past" when there were no separate countries, only "Korea."

Put simply, until recently when Japan and South Korea's apologetic exchange began to crumble apart over the tiny islands between them, Seoul's acquiescence to Tokyo's words further weakened the demands of South Korean citizens that Japan recognize their histories. Since 1965, Japan and South Korea's officially shared "remorse" for "the past" has constrained history's parameters, rather than expand them. Both governments have tried to maintain a calm that may make sense regarding diplomacy, business, or military games but has little to do with history in terms of finding out what happened to whom, what, when, and where. Officials, however, have smoothed things over in the name of history—Harry Harootunian's "ruse" mentioned earlier—confusing for everyone and especially themselves what is really involved.

In the 1990s, the intensity of claims against Japan entrenched the divide between those saying Japan had never apologized for its past in Korea and those saying it had. The victims and their supporters who found Japan's words lacking in meaning often overlooked their government's agreement to them or, and maybe more to the point, found it *as* difficult to challenge their own leaders. Rather than consider how these conditions might relate to how those asking for apology made their demands, however—which would be one way to approach the problem historically—this only made Japan's anti-apology apologists angrier and more politicized. As of today, the movement against "remorse" on Japan's part seeks to deny the increasingly rare survivors of Japan's historical violence the dignity of even listening to their stories.

In March 1999, Prime Minister Obuchi and President Kim cele-
brated the six-month anniversary of their written "joint declaration" with an unusual live TV broadcast. No journalist raised the
dreaded issue of "the past," and neither did Obuchi or Kim. Instead, they spoke of the dawn of a "new history," nodding to business and military leaders to forge ahead under the rubric of "cultural
sharing." For some, the expression rather startlingly evoked Japan's
official policy in Korea during the 1920s, which was called "cultural
rule."[38]

Historical echoes notwithstanding, the South Korean government lived up to President Kim's commitment to "cultural sharing"
and began lifting the nation's fifty-three-year ban on Japanese music and film. Of course, bootlegs, pirated copies, and underground
exchange had long kept savvy Koreans aware of what was hot in
Tokyo well before the Internet made it all seem so matter-of-fact,
but to do this earlier was harder than many might imagine. As a result, in the spring of 2000, for example, it was still quite exciting in
Seoul or Busan to see a Japanese movie on the big screen, or at least
it was for the first time since 1945. And regardless of protests over
the islands, the comfort women, and Japan's shrine to war dead,
Japanese popular culture remains a multimillion dollar industry in
South Korea.

For its part, the Japanese government actively began promoting
tourism to South Korea, "so near and yet so far," and planned ex-
travagant arts and academic exchange programs.[39] In 2002, Tokyo
and Seoul co-hosted soccer's World Cup. Both countries' teams
performed better than expected, with history's underdogs, the
Koreans, doing just enough better than the Japanese—but not too
much—for almost everyone to feel good.

This elaborately manufactured good feeling blended seamlessly
into an Asia-wide craze for South Korean TV shows and movies,
known by the Chinese-coined term as the "Korean Wave." In April
2003, one swell of the wave brought *Winter Sonata* to Japan. This
TV series of star-crossed love caused nothing less than widespread

FIGURE 2.1 Korean soccer fans, June 2002 (*Korea Herald*)

hysteria among middle-aged, middle-class Japanese women for its leading man, Bae Yong-joon, who became fondly known in Japanese as "Yon-sama."[40]

Thousands caused a stampede at Tokyo's Haneda airport in April 2004 when Bae arrived for a visit, sending twelve women to the hospital. When he flew home, Japanese women desperate for love jammed flights to Seoul. Scores made Korean matchmaking companies instantly rich, seeking Korean men for marriage and disparaging their Japanese options in "Yon-sama's" name.[41] A Korean friend of mine rented her condo in the Chunchon ski resort area where the series was filmed to a succession of Japanese fans for more money than she ever imagined.[42] Bloggers had a field day, and one Online culture critic declared, "It's not an exaggeration to say that *Winter Sonata* has done more politically for South Korea and Japan than the FIFA World Cup."[43]

With such a high, however, the crash could almost be expected, and by 2005 one of the most popular books in Japan was titled *Hating the Korean Wave*.[44] The *Hating* book itself is preoccupied with South Korea, yet the broader social backlash that propelled it gathered steam not simply because the "Yon-sama" pandemonium was so over the top; by coincidence, South Korea's popular culture wave crashed on Japanese shores roughly at the time that a series of stunning

FIGURE 2.2 Bae Yong-joon,
actor in the Korean television series
Winter Sonata (*Aera* magazine)

provocations by North Korean leader Kim Jong-il were realizing
their effects in Japanese society. In simplest terms—and similar to
how 9/11 collapsed many Americans' perceptions of Middle East-
erners into all one category—by the end of 2004, as news from
Pyongyang became stranger and stranger, the "Yon-sama" phenomenon more and more frenzied, and, on top of it all, the island
dispute took off again, some Japanese warped everything and everyone Korean into one group that was, by definition, a threat to
being Japanese.

Whereas, for most Americans, North Korea's nuclear weapons
program is the root cause of mistrust with Pyongyang, for Japanese it
is what is known as the "abduction issue" (*rachi mondai*). Beginning in

the 1970s, the North Korean government began kidnapping Japanese citizens to North Korea to work as language instructors to train spies to infiltrate Japan, an idea, some believe, originated by the national leader Kim Jong-il. It is said that more than twenty or fifty or maybe even one hundred innocent Japanese were its victims.

What we know for certain is that, in September 2002, Japanese Prime Minister Koizumi traveled to Pyongyang for the first head of state meeting ever to begin "normalizing" relations with North Korea along the lines of its relations with South Korea.

An apology for the "unfortunate past" and financial incentives were to be part of the deal.[45] During the meeting, however, Kim Jong-il acknowledged his government's involvement in the kidnapping program, and Koizumi returned to Tokyo with the news that North Korea had admitted abducting thirteen people; eight were dead, and five remained there. Profound shock and despair engulfed Japan.

FIGURE 2.3 Japanese prime minister Koizumi Junichiro and North Korean leader Kim Jong-il, September 2002 (*Tokyo Shimbun*)

Lost in the moment, Pyongyang's disclosure about the kidnappings came in the form of an official apology. This rare instance of "double apology"—Tokyo to Pyongyang for colonization and Pyongyang to Tokyo for the abductions—is perhaps unique in recent international relations and raised several very important factors about political apologies, all of which disappeared in the maelstrom caused by North Korea's revelation.

First, regardless of whether Prime Minister Koizumi should be remembered for his repeated visits to the Yasukuni Shrine, for trying to disband state-controlled postal savings accounts, or for grabbing Lisa Marie Presley at Graceland and singing "Love Me Tender," he broke with decades of constipated official Japanese policy toward North Korea and decided to get on with things with Pyongyang once and for all. To the palpable anger of many in his own conservative party, Koizumi flew to North Korea armed with the formula of "sorrow and remorse for the unfortunate past." This act did nothing but underscore that the content of that past—meaning history—had very little to do with the apology offered for it.

Second, regardless of whether North Korean leader Kim Jong-il should be thought of as the diabolical playboy that numerous American news magazines have portrayed him as, or, as he sees himself, surrounded by throngs of adoring countrymen, during his 2002 meeting with Koizumi, Kim clearly understood that political apologies were the name of the game. He offered Koizumi a perfectly scripted counter of "regret for the deaths of eight of the victims," making these quid pro quo apologies highlight their sheer instrumentality. Kim's apologies also begged the question of whether a "double apology" would work like a double negative, erasing what the other had said.

At the time, however, any critical examination of these apologies or related ones remained at the level of excited talk—and maybe even only between my colleagues and me—because, within the month, Kim Jong-il owned up to his nation's nuclear weapons program and placed Pyongyang beyond the pale for many Japanese and Americans. Even though some might think that the nuclear weapons issue might have then become *the* cause of concern in Japan because of its proximity to North Korea, Japanese remained transfixed on the abductions. And even though there has been growing fatigue with the issue, and even after North Korea tested a weapon in October 2006, the abduction matter continues to predominate Japanese discussions about North Korea.[46] In January 2007, for example, the Japanese government sponsored special film showings as well as other events about the issue at the United Nations in New York just as its new secretary general, South Korean Ban Ki-moon, took charge. The reason that the abduction issue remains *the* story in Japan is fairly straightforward. Its immediate human dimension generates almost total national sympathy. More important, however, Pyongyang's nuclear weapons program is far less useful than the kidnappings for summoning the myth of Japanese togetherness. Superficially at least, the kidnappings do not raise certain questions; for example, "Would Japanese cities or the U.S. military bases in Japan be North Korea's target?" Or, "Why does Pyongyang hate Japan so much?" Even quick answers quickly spiral backward into the open-ended mess of history.

Moreover, the abduction question came with its own baggage in the Japanese political and media worlds that made anyone and everyone earning a living off public opinion feel the need to be heard or seen claiming the victims in the name of Japan when North Korea came clean. In the 1970s, when the mysterious disappearances began, the victims' families approached the Japanese government for help, but they were told that their children had simply run away. Much information is still needed about who in the Japanese government knew what and when, yet what is known is that ever since the kidnappings started, government spokesmen and most of the media (except the right-wing *Sankei Shimbun* for its own North Korean bashing purposes) continued to ignore the families' requests for information or publicity for their plight. They occasionally accused them of lying or of being spies themselves.

As a result, when Kim Jong-il confessed to his government's official involvement in the plan, and it was clear that the Japanese government and press had not protected its own, every politician and media outlet in Japan leapt on the story, especially liberal-leaning ones like the *Asahi* to atone for their earlier lack of attention. On some days, there has been no other story. Millions of people openly wept watching the survivors' homecoming on live TV in October 2002. They wept again the following spring when the victims' teenage children who were born and raised in North Korea were "returned" to Japan. For some, the issue of the children's "return" to Japan raised discussions about the power of the verb "to come home" which, in Japanese, uses the word "country" for "home." How could the victims' children be "coming home" to a place that they never even knew until recently was vaguely a part of them? It is no surprise, however, given the stakes involved, that the defenders of a homogeneous Japan prevailed, and the Korean-born, Korean-raised, Korean-speaking children's blood won hands down over any other

FIGURE 2.4 The kidnapped Japanese return,
October 2002 (*Korea Herald*)

issue of Japanese identity. This remains an important notion, given that being even "half" Japanese, for example, is never enough for many Japanese-born, Japanese-raised, Japanese-speaking Japanese-Koreans who *want* to be defined as Japanese. Needless to say, skeptics were and are viewed as less than Japanese.

The kidnap victims stayed in Japan for good when they came back in October 2002.

Throughout the fall, Japanese obsessively watched the effects of their so-called North Korean brainwashing vanish. All five got new haircuts and clothes in Tokyo bureaucratic-chic. Some took quite well to the style, eventually getting jobs in local administrative offices and in schools where they started to teach, of all things, the Korean language to Japanese students. The victims resumed their full and, arguably, divinely appointed Japanese-ness over the 2003 New Year's holiday when they had their first chance in decades to pray at local shrines. Television cameras followed their every move, and the message was clear: the stain of North Korea was gone.

The only person involved in the whole abduction scheme that Japanese cannot wholly incorporate as one of their own is Charles Robert Jenkins, the American-born husband of one of the Japanese victims. In 1965, Jenkins defected to North Korea while serving in the American military along the demilitarized zone in South Korea, and his appearance in the mix caused all kinds of additional problems. The abduction story broke on the eve of the U.S. invasion of Iraq, and at that moment the American military was not about to pardon any of its soldiers who had run off to the "commie North" to avoid Vietnam, which is what the military would have had to do for Jenkins to enable him to join his Japanese wife in Japan. The extradition laws that exist between Japan and the United States would have required that Jenkins be immediately arrested and sent "home."[47]

When Jenkins' wife returned to Japan with the four others in October 2002, Jenkins and their two children stayed in Pyongyang. Eventually, Tokyo and Washington and Pyongyang worked out a deal. Jenkins and his wife would reunite in Jakarta, where Jenkins would receive medical treatments unavailable to him in Pyongyang. Because Jakarta is, according to international law, what is called a "third country"—meaning that no one *really* responsible would have to take responsibility for what was going on—from there Charles Jenkins could finally come to Japan together with their two daughters. Unlike the other victims' children, the Jenkins girls, from birth, were defined as "half" in North Korea, as they also would be in Japan.

When Jenkins, his daughters, and his wife were reunited as a family in July 2004, the Japanese media and its pundits had yet another chance to monopolize the airwaves for several days discussing what it meant to be Japanese or, in this case, what it meant to be *not* Japanese. Japanese news cameras at Jakarta's international airport beamed home the first blip of Jenkins's plane coming into view. Reporters built up as much suspense as possible until the plane door opened, and the slight, white-haired, sixty-four-year-old man limped down the stairs with a cane, whereupon he immediately embraced his wife. They then fell into a loving and eager kiss on the lips for all in Japan to see. "They're kissing! They're kissing!" each major station's reporter shouted as if the gesture would be lost without translation. "Jenkins has given his wife a kiss! They're kissing! It's an American kiss!"

When I heard this, I quickly flipped through the TV channels to make sure that other reporters were similarly fixated, and I remember thinking, "What? What are they talking about?" I was struck not because I thought the comment was anti-this or anti-that but because my own stereotypes were at odds with those of the Japanese reporters. Before the reporters said anything, I was thinking to myself, "Wow, the Jenkinses have become pretty Korean." I thought this blatantly stereotypical thought, because husband and wife repeatedly stroked each other's faces while kissing in the way that I have grown accustomed to seeing people kiss in Seoul when they are desperate to see each other or as Korean family members are featured when South Korean TV shows them reuniting after decades of living on opposite sides of the demilitarized zone.

The more I thought about everyone's preconceptions and preoccupations (my own included) and about affection and national identity, the more I realized that the significant point in all this was that coverage of this moment ran absolutely counter to Japan's whole *Winter Sonata* craze. If nothing else, the "Yon-sama" phenomenon revolved around a soap opera about love, separation, assumed identity, and plenty of kissing on the lips. What had everyone been watching?

An interesting note is that when the kidnapping story first broke, South Koreans paid almost no attention. On one level, the very subject of kidnapping remains too sensitive in domestic Korean affairs, because both South and North Korea have kidnapped hundreds of each other's nationals since the Korean War ended in 1953, not to mention the problem of POWs who were not allowed to go home on either side. On a deeper level, however, it is difficult for any Korean to comprehend how the tragic stories of five individuals could so eclipse everything else in Japan when the Japanese government has yet to deal with the tragic stories of the millions of Asian lives ruined by the forced separations and abductions perpetrated by its colonial and wartime government.

Misguided or not, North Korean leader Kim Jong-il's bewildering behavior should be understood as an attempt to generate legitimacy for himself abroad and at home—international legitimacy by coming clean with Japan about the abduction scheme, and domestic legitimacy by standing up to the United States and pursuing nuclear weapons. Without a doubt, though, his contributions to the growing anti-Korean feeling in Japan since 2002 have shifted Japanese popular consciousness about North Korea from suspicion to outrage. Most alarming, his actions have enabled ideologues on Japan's Right, such as the popular governor of Tokyo Ishihara Shintaro, to make their racist commentary make increasing common sense to many. During the past few years, people like Ishihara have even generated mainstream support for some of the more extreme acts that their hate mongering has produced, such as beating up kids of Korean descent on their way to school or once again defaming as "anti-Japanese" those who demonstrate interest in the historical reasons behind these issues.[48] Most notorious, of course, was the September 2003 firebombing of the house of a prominent Japanese foreign ministry official for his efforts to talk to North Koreans.[49]

These recent moments of extreme fondness and hate underscore the profound disconnect between Japan and Korea that remains at the heart of what lingers from history that no popular wave can wash away. Many Japanese will continue to hate Korea openly and without hesitation because the inner histories of being Japanese and being Korean remain so absent from Japan's social landscape. It will still be easy and fun to fly to Seoul for a weekend shopping spree as long as you don't have to bring any history "home," just as it will be preferable to keep Koreans safely inside your TV set because there they do not disturb being Japanese.

"IN THANKS TO YOU ALL!!"

Beyond the loving and hating Korea waves, Kobayashi Yoshinori can claim more responsibility than anyone for popularizing the trend to discredit those who would apologize for any of modern Japan's history. He is a cartoonist and a pundit, and the astronomical sales of his two most famous books, *Sensōron* (On War) in 1998 and its successor *Sensōron 2* in 2001, attest to his central place in this endeavor.[50]

In these books, Kobayashi repeatedly explains that failure to praise those who fought for Japan's empire created a "masochistic" understanding of history in which Japan and Japanese remain judged for what foreigners determined to be crimes. To his mind, the nation's sell-outs perpetuate this "masochistic" view by demanding apologies for three events: Japan's "so-called war of aggression," colonization of Korea, and apparent "troubles" (*meiwaku*) Japan caused in Asia. According to Kobayashi, since 1945 Japanese "leftists," "intellectuals," "individualists," "cultists," and, above all, "the media" are responsible for this treachery, and "the Americans" have played no small part.[51]

Presenting history like using a remote control, Kobayashi invites readers into his narrative by drawing himself as the main character, wearing either an Imperial Army uniform (as on the covers of his books) or an "I could be you" plain, black sweater. Just to make sure readers know where he stands, randomly in the text he includes drawings of himself at his desk or in bed being embraced by a pretty, young, and completely naked Japanese woman. In an unusual spin on the erotic displays that typify Japanese comics, the naked woman (or women) clinging to Kobayshi will have to wait, however, because Japanese history must first be satisfied.[52]

Taking Kobayashi Yoshinori seriously only gives him more attention, yet thoughtful critics have argued that to ignore his work is more than intellectual snobbery; it is cowardice.[53] Put differently, to step around the Kobayashi phenomenon is akin to pretending that Bill O'Reilly of Fox News is irrelevant to today's America.[54] It is no surprise that both Kobayashi and O'Reilly manipulate similar views of history, reducing everything in their paths to the least common denominator, playing on the assumption that a fact is a fact if you, the reader, are vaguely familiar with some of the particulars. Both also rely on similarly charged masculine contours of right and wrong—"feminists" are an especially loathsome threat to the "truth" and "values"—and both find no logical inconsistency with defaming their opponents as "idiots" or "fanatics" while relying on imaginary evidence to support their own claims.[55]

Throughout his books, Kobayashi reworks the long-standing tactics of Japanese extremists into matter-of-fact storytelling by reworking demands for an "apology" (shazai/謝罪) for Japan's record during World War II into demands for "gratitude" (kansha/感謝) for those who endured it. In the first volume he clarifies the objects of his hatred, and describes his plan for rescuing Japan's honor in a five-panel drawing, the text of which reads:

For our grandfathers who endured the brutal war with all their might and perished, for our grandfathers who achieved victory on the battlefield of honor, for our grandfathers who endured the even more unendurable after the war when Japan's military was reviled, for our grandfathers who hold grudges against the mindless beatings they endured in the military, for our grandmothers who narrowly held down the home front during the war, and for the comfort women who gave comfort to Japanese troops, I'LL TELL THE STORY OF THE WAR IN THANKS TO YOU ALL!![56]

FIGURE 2.5 Poster advertising "Day of Gratitude"
(Nippon no Kai)

Given the levels to which Kobayashi's work aspires, it is predict-
able that he takes his cue from various extremist groups who also
urge "giving thanks," such as the poster from one such organization
pictured here that has renamed Japan's surrender date as a "Day of
Gratitude."

Kobayashi rehashes much of the same story in the second volume,
yet he makes much more of the significance—in positive terms—of
Japan's having fought a "holy war" in the name of "Greater Asia." To
this end, he even delayed the book's publication to include the 9/11
attacks on the United States into his explanation that Japanese
should be proud of their nation's historical and "spiritually based"
attempts to "liberate" Asia from white rule.[57] As a result, the second

volume is nothing less than a mass-marketed manifesto for Japan's anti-apology apologists. In it, Kobayashi argues that the government's conservative establishment sold out the country during the 1990s by even responding to calls for apology. And unlike the pre-1990s apologists of Japan's wartime record who would simply ignore the existence of survivors of Japan's wartime atrocities such as the comfort women, Kobayashi unabashedly includes them in his logic to keep his own narrative as current as possible.

After a lengthy discussion targeting Japan's 1991–93 prime minister, Miyazawa Kiichi, for his weakness on this score (as Kobayashi sees it)—in one drawing Kobayashi lops off Miyazawa's skull cap as well as that of a foreign ministry spokesman to demonstrate their "empty-headedness" as they "apologize six times and express remorse twice!"—Kobayashi draws the root cause of this apparently idiotic behavior: a self-satisfied, healthy-looking young woman surrounded by cash flowing from heaven. This figure is meant to portray a former comfort woman at the end of the war, and the text explains, "Because it was a war-zone and dangerous, the money was great. There were lots of them who earned more than 10 times what a college graduate did in those days and 100 times more than a soldier. In 2–3 years they built houses back in their hometowns."[58] Just in case this explanation is too vague, on the right-hand side of the drawing, silhouettes of soldiers (presumably Japanese) race head-on into explosions while female figures on the other side (presumably like the young woman or as she will be in the future) walk away unscathed with bundles and bags of what must be the money tumbling down.

Volumes of documentary evidence that appeared during the 1990s prove Kobayashi's explanation of the Japanese wartime comfort women system wrong. Nonetheless, Kobayashi deploys a striking, young, and foreign face to counter the numerous pictures of the system's actual young women that surfaced then—one of the better-known ones is reprinted here—and to cast doubt on the testimonies that elderly survivors were giving in Japan at the time.

Kobayashi frames his outrageous ideas in the middle of a diatribe against the centrist and, by their own definition, pragmatic politicians who had apologized to Korea in some measure, cul-

Who controls memory? .

FIGURE 2.6 Former comfort women and soldiers
(United States Army Archives)

minating in a demand to "Make Insulting the Nation a Crime! Put
(the Politicians) Who Insulted Japan and the Japanese People in
Jail!"[59]

With similar drawings and text throughout the book's hundreds
of pages, Kobayashi willfully tries to court today's young Japanese
who, at the time these texts were published, were living through the
nation's worst economic moments since the early 1950s. The logic is
simple: they are here to take our money again.

YET ANOTHER APOLOGY

The July 2003 issue of Japan's best-selling literary journal, *Bungei
Shunjū*, printed "Imperial Apology to the People" across its cover,
and inside it reprinted a copy of a newly found 1948 document pur-
porting to be Hirohito's thoughts on apology.[60] Nonfiction author
Kato Kyoko found the document among Tajima Michiji's personal
effects, and Tajima had been head of the Imperial Household

Agency and Hirohito's confidant. Kato defines the written note as the wartime emperor's apology, and suggests that it could "broadly recast a page of Showa history (1926–1989)," referring to the long-standing discussion of Japan's war responsibility, the emperor, and apology for Japan's rampage and defeat in Asia and the Pacific during the first half of the twentieth century.[61]

Never mind the obvious problems, however. Never mind, for example, that the former emperor apologized in language that required a Japanese translator, who himself was Japanese, to render it comprehensible in popularly used Japanese. Never mind that Hirohito did not write the document himself; likely, he expressed his thoughts to Tajima, in whose private records Kato made her discovery. And, most important, never mind that Hirohito did not apologize to the people who have been seeking redress all these years since 1945. Instead, he expressed "deep shame" to his *non*-colonial subjects, paying particular attention to those "who lost their property abroad."[62]

For many Japanese, these words of Japan's dead emperor would describe Hirohito as *always and already* apologetic. The people who claim that they still deserve an apology remain ostracized, and this discovery in the end simply shades the history of Japan's empire and war in the same halftones that has long obscured its victims' stories.[63] In the logic of those determined never to allow the record of Japan's state-run terror from staining Japanese history writ large, however, the tragic wartime leader did, in fact, apologize. End of story.

Hirohito's words will surely continue to emerge from the grave. If they do so along their current path, they may only reintroduce for younger or forgetful Japanese the apologetic sentiment the emperor expressed in 1946 when he renounced his divinity: "The devastation of the war inflicted upon our cities, the miseries of the destitute, the stagnation of trade, shortage of food, and the great and growing number of the unemployed are indeed heart-rending." It would seem, then, that the "Chrysanthemum Taboo" continues to define Japanese identity at the cost of its history.

CHAPTER THREE

Illegal Japan

Korean national identity incorporates a widespread belief these days that Japan must still apologize for the colonization of Korea (1905–1945). A significant point is that this belief rests on an understanding that Japanese control was not just traumatic, it was illegal. It is a passion that weaves in and out of current events, becoming almost religiously empowered when the details of history get caught up in the storms of conviction.

In March 2006, thousands of Koreans gathered in Seoul and set fire to a cardboard mock-up of Japan's Ministry of Education building to protest recently published Japanese school textbooks that named the disputed islands Japanese. The following month, when two Japanese Coast Guard ships approached the islands "to conduct research" on the area's sea floor, South Korea's president, Roh Moo-hyun, declared that Japan had learned nothing from its imperialist past and was trying to restart its forty-year illegal domination of Korea. On live TV he vowed that, for Korea, "this is a matter where no surrender or compromise is possible," and he then allocated $35 million of the national budget for development of the islands' resources. By the time Japan recalled its ships, the *Kaíyo* and *Meíyo*, the South Korean Navy had positioned eighteen ships of its own to protect the islands, and Pyongyang promised unprecedented cooperation. Koreans were again on the streets and in Internet chat rooms protesting Japan's actions, and some took the meaning of "offshore bank account" to a new level by depositing the equivalent of $5 million into the cyber Dokdo branch of the Daegu Bank to stake Korean ownership. Seoul's foreign ministry created a task force to convince the world of Korea's legal claim to the islands, and a man named Yang Bong-ho even tried to kill himself to defend his country's honor.

Describing a nation's past as horrendous is one thing but calling it illegal is another. There is no doubt that Japan brutally governed Korea during the first half of the twentieth century. Widely known stories follow the contours of rule by violence anywhere, and include torture, forced labor, random killing, confiscation of property, abduction, rape, forced conscription, censorship, imprisonment, forced religious conversion, forced name changes, and forced language use. Even those in Japan today who overlook much of the twentieth century with amazing ease describe this period of history with a baseline acknowledgment of the bad: "We did good things, too." There won't ever be a final death count, because volumes of records were destroyed or lost. Stacks of published materials provide overwhelming evidence that many Japanese, and many Koreans working for them, committed heinous acts ruining the lives of millions. But proving this is not really the point anymore. Considering the extremes that Koreans go to *now* to protest anything echoing the era of Japanese rule—Koreans who with increasing exception were not even alive at the time—something more must be at stake in declaring this part of the national past illegal.

In important ways, this determination and focus has much to do with ongoing global social inequalities and is far from unique to Korea. For roughly the last two decades, from about the time the Berlin Wall fell and Emperor Hirohito died, postcolonial and post-imperial movements and governments around the world from Australia to Nigeria have found common voice in describing their nation's historical experience of colonization in terms of criminal victimization—including the crime of genocide—that must now be brought to justice through apology and reparations in national or international courts of law. In June 2000, Algerian President Abdelaziz Bouteflika added an important new dimension to this movement by challenging the world to agree that the "debt of former colonial powers towards their former colonies . . . is beyond any statute of limitations."[1]

Calling the Japanese era illegal thus engages Koreans with this international trend, which helps explain much of its immediate fervor. Equally important, however, is to examine some very Korean details of this phenomenon in order to understand what is at stake for Koreans today.

THE ERA OF JAPANESE RULE

The South and North Korean governments describe the era of Japanese rule in ways that reveal how each claims legitimacy today. Pyongyang uses an angrier expression for this shared past, which more than anything else focuses on how Seoul, by comparison, seems calm in its official protests against Japan.

Koreans generally refer to "Japanese times" or "Japanese colonial times," or talk about "when the Japanese were here," and almost everyone will tell you that the whole era was "illegal." Both the South and North Korean governments use these words, too, yet with an important difference: Seoul most often describes 1905–1945 as the "colonial period," whereas Pyongyang calls it an era of "military occupation." This distinction might appear trivial or meaningless to some, and many South Koreans prefer and use North Korea's choice of words. But their government has not regularly used the expression "military occupation" during the past several decades, because the words alone would disrupt the pattern of relations Seoul agreed to with Tokyo in 1965 and, more pressing, would lay bare the problem of America's ongoing troop presence in South Korea.

The demilitarized zone (DMZ) that runs across Korea might seem unrelated to Japanese rule, because it marks the end of the Korean War (1950–1953). This strip of land, however, closely approximates the line that two young American Army officers, Dean Rusk and Charles Bonesteel, drew across a map of Korea in the middle of the night on August 10–11, 1945.[2] Following America's atomic bombings of Hiroshima (August 6) and Nagasaki (August 9) and the Soviet Union's declaration of war on Japan (August 8), Rusk and Bonesteel took thirty minutes to designate the American and Soviet spheres of occupation in Korea which the United States decided would follow Japan's surrender (August 15). To the Americans' surprise, the Soviets agreed without negotiation, but no one was as surprised as the Koreans since no Korean knew that this enormous act of geographical management was taking place.

The American decision to divide Korea remains striking if only because so many Americans have no idea of their nation's responsibility for doing so. Seeing this decision through more recent history makes it difficult to get at this past, a point well-intentioned students make clear to me every year in Korean history class, when they say, "Oh, I thought it was because of the North Koreans." The division is also remarkable from another perspective: as a result of America's actions, Japan's surrender yielded a North and South Korea and not a North and South Japan—like an East and West Germany—yet Japan had been at war with the Allies, whereas Korea had been a Japanese colony, legally incapable of declaring war on anybody.

Even more confusing from today's perspective is that America did not consider Korea to have strategic value at the time. In November 1943, the future of what would become of Japan's empire took shape at the Cairo Conference, and Franklin D. Roosevelt took charge of Korea. He viewed Korea's path in the then prevailing liberal terms of cultivating independent societies through various stages of development, determining that Korea's independence would come via trusteeship, a form of political coaching to teach the Koreans how to have their own country. Ironically, Roosevelt's ideas echoed those the Japanese used to justify their takeover of Korea in

FIGURE 3.1 U.S. postage stamp, 1944
(United States Postal Service)

the first place, and they are not too distant from American planning for Iraq today.

Washington was confident, then, in its newly emerging role as liberator of the world and began celebrating as much during the summer of 1943 with the "Overrun Nations" postage stamp series that sought to make Americans mindful of the countries that U.S. soldiers and sailors fought to free abroad while Americans mailed their letters at home. In what can be seen as one of the United States' first open challenges to Japan's 1910 annexation of Korea, in November 1944 Korea found a place for itself on a stamp in this series.

The stamp's rising phoenix and female figure breaking the bonds of servitude are great period graphics, yet two less obvious features make it even more interesting. First, the United States had been an ardent champion of Japan's takeover of Korea when it happened at the beginning of the twentieth century. Not for a minute did any American official protest that Japan was "overrunning" the country then, and, as Japan tightened its control, with the exception of two or three missionaries, the overwhelming majority of American politicians, pundits, scholars, and theologians nodded in agreement with the *New York Tribune*'s July 1908 praise for Japan's actions: "The Law of survival of the fittest prevails among states as well as among plants and animals. [K]orea has been conspicuously unfit." Second, Korea was the only non-European country—the only nonwhite place in the world for that matter—to merit mention as an "overrun nation" in the 1943–44 stamp series, demonstrating America's confusion

American hypocrisy

about its own occupation of the Philippines and Hawaii, or that of its Allied compatriots in Southeast Asia. It is significant, of course, that Washington never hesitated to describe Japan's imperialist ambitions in this very same region as treacherous and even subhuman.

The American ability to deny an American empire spanned the twentieth century and is moving healthily into the twenty-first. Historian Bruce Cumings noticed how this feature of American self-narration played out in Roosevelt's Korea policy, observing FDR's repeated mention at Cairo of the success of American "benevolence towards the Filipinos" to justify delayed independence for Korea.[3] Cumings explains that, in the Korean case, this enduring American characteristic required "overlook[ing] the darker aspects of the American record in the Philippines, particularly the three years of counterinsurgency necessary to establish American dominance in the first place. It also overlooked the simple fact that the peoples of Indochina, Korea, Malaya, and elsewhere did not contemplate a patient wait for independence after Japan's defeat."[4]

Thus, in 1945, with the "overrun" Korea stamp in circulation, America added post-Japan Korea as a non-colonial colony to its own empire through the trusteeship scheme, making it the first neo-colony of the post Second World War terrain, and the Soviets agreed to their share. Soviet soldiers began attacking Japanese-controlled Korean cities in the north of the country on August 8 when Moscow declared war on Japan, so it was relatively simple for them to expand south toward the American line at the 38th parallel, following Tokyo's surrender on August 15.[5] As of late August, the twenty-five million Koreans who survived the period of Japanese rule began to find themselves free of the Japanese, yet living among Russian or American soldiers depending on where they were.

Regardless of the foreign troops, however, Koreans immediately organized political committees to establish their own government on their own soil for the first time in half a century. Possibilities spanned from radical communism to the reverse-gazing desires of the once nobly titled landlords. The committees in the Soviet-controlled north moved quickly, and, by early 1946, they were organizing institutions and land redistribution. By the following summer, there was a growing economy and a functioning political party with a single leader, the anti-Japanese fighter Kim Il Sung.[6] In the south, however, Washington viewed even the existence of such people's committees with fear and instead anointed men who would fall into lock step with America's growing obsession with containing communism. In turn, these men took advantage of Washington's cash and complacency, brutalizing their opponents and their supporters.

Through a series of unfortunate events—chief among them General MacArthur's decision to let the Chinese nationalist leader Chiang Kai-shek name a Korean that America could "count on"— Syngman Rhee won the starring role of serving U.S. interests, making the whole moment further prefigure post-invasion Iraq today. Similar to the choice of Ahmed Chalabi in America's first attempt at "letting Iraqis rule," for example, Syngman Rhee had been in the United States for much of the Japanese era and spoke English better than Korean by the time the Americans brought him "home" to a place where he had no political base.

Blended into Moscow's and Washington's different approaches to controlling Korea were the fates of the Koreans who had been most entwined with the hated Japanese. In 1945, Kim Il Sung proudly wore his anti-Japanese credentials, his megalomania notwithstanding. At thirty-three years of age, his charismatic call to lead Koreans out of their suffering resonated broadly, and because the Soviets allowed the people's committees to function in their area, the purge trials that Kim and his comrades orchestrated shaped the northern Korean landscape following Japan's defeat. Unsurprisingly, Kim and his fellow guerilla fighters were fairly brutal to those who had worked with the Japanese colonizers, and thousands fled south or abroad if they could, and often with new names.

In the south, the pickled-prune-like Syngman Rhee was ostensibly anti-Japanese, yet he had so much difficulty gaining control that he hired Korean thugs who had previously worked for the Japanese police to imprison or murder his opponents. Just as bad, he intervened in all the attempts in the south to hold purge trials or make

related policy because the only Koreans he could bribe for support
with his budget of American assistance were those already most en-
riched and made powerful by the Japanese. Thus, during Rhee's
early reign of terror, this particularly distasteful group of people es-
caped persecution and redefined themselves and became defined in
the south as the new, true Koreans. Regardless of what these people
may have believed individually or privately at the time, their public
praise for the United States—especially the U.S. military—became
their binding common denominator.

On August 15, 1948, instead of holding nationwide elections,
America helped sponsor Rhee's elevation to the presidency of the
First Republic of Korea, bringing a new nation into being (South
Korea) that claimed sovereignty over all of Korea and yet was able to
control only half. In response, the Democratic People's Republic of
Korea announced itself in Pyongyang, on September 9, 1948, bringing North Korea into being, which similarly claimed to govern the
whole country. The Americans and Soviets packed to leave, something that proved a lot easier for the Russians, who, unlike the
Americans, had not created a separate authority for themselves. The
occupiers' collective departure, however, triggered Seoul and Pyongyang's bipolar views of history and governance into a civil war
(1950–1953), which was made all the worse by the foreign militaries
that poured back in. Over one in eight Koreans alive died, yet neither
side could claim victory. The renewed dividing line has defined the
armistice and Korea itself until now.

In the clearest terms, Korea's division results directly from its
twentieth-century encounters with Japan and the United States,
which is essential to remember whenever thinking about present-day
interaction between Japan, Korea, and the United States. Korean
unification remains an essential element of Northeast Asian and
global security, and failure to work for it now will only necessitate
the need to justify this short-sightedness in the future. Put differently, it creates even more history problems.

One significant way that Seoul defines itself in control of Korea today
is by narrating the nation's Japanese past as its "colonial" experience.

Although South Koreans have run South Korea throughout its history, the precarious nature of the state's early legitimacy and the even more precarious nature of its post-1953 survival have made those in charge deeply dependent on their American backers. Whether or not South Korea is technically an American colony is not the point, because America exerts imperial power there regardless. The roughly thirty thousand American troops on the ground, in the air, and in South Korea's oceans make this clear to everyone in daily life and points to a very real difference between post-1953 South and North Korea until now: although there is continuing talk about reducing American troops and giving Seoul more control over its military decisions, the Americans are *still* there, whereas the Russians and Chinese left the North more than fifty years ago.

North Korea's leaders and its media have long leapt on this state of affairs, routinely describing South Korea as an American-occupied puppet regime. Thus, when Pyongyang uses the term "military occupation" for the era of Japanese rule, it does so knowing that South Korean officials cannot use the same expression for the same past. For Seoul to describe the period from 1905 to 1945 in these terms would be simultaneously to agree—at least in part—with Pyongyang that South Korea has been under U.S. military occupation since 1953, which would discredit any South Korean claim to sovereignty over anything.

Pyongyang's gamble, however, has been just as tenuous as Seoul's, and, given the state's current humanitarian crisis, is now simply disgraceful. Working under the assumption that North Koreans and anyone else would comprehend "military occupation" only as a foreign intrusion, the nation's scriptwriters prevent North Koreans from expressing or conceiving that Pyongyang has increasingly ruled through a military occupation of itself.

Kim Il Sung's 1994 death came on top of dwindling Russian fuel supplies (following the 1989 collapse of the Soviet Union) as well as new relations with a reforming China, all of which combined to destabilize his son's, Kim Jong-il's, early days of inherited rule. Since the mid-1990s, more than one million North Koreans have routinely served in the nation's People's Army out of a population of roughly twenty million, and mandatory male conscription has increased to over a decade. Although North Korea's ongoing famine shifts these numbers around, Kim Jong-il's government only further militarizes the country. Soldiers and their families continue to eat, and since 2003 the state has openly promoted a "Military First!" policy, with slogans and songs reminiscent of imperial Japan in the 1930s. Although a few senior North Korean officers have defected during the past decade, most in the military appear at worst neutral about their privileges because there is no mass mutiny going on. If there were, things would change fast, since the military runs the country hand in hand with Kim Jong-il.

In strangely reinforcing ways, therefore, South and North Korea officially obfuscate their currently divided existence by the way they refer to their shared Japanese past. They agree that the era was illegal and continue to demand apologies and reparations for it from Japan. Although Seoul forfeits the more punishing expression of "military occupation" that it might hurl at Tokyo, it publicly diverts the nature of South Korea's ongoing existence with the United States by avoiding the expression. For its part, Pyongyang confuses only those who have no other information—its own people—governing now solely through military force while condemning Japan for having done so one hundred years ago.

A FIELD OF DREAMS

At the beginning of the twentieth century, many Koreans tried to protest Japan's takeover of their country. Some even denounced it as illegal at the time. Once Japan formally annexed Korea in 1910, however, the colonial government freely censured everything and anything that crossed its path. With the important exception of the 1919 spontaneous mass anti-Japanese uprisings, for the most part throughout the era of Japanese rule, those who wanted to defy Japan openly—to call it illegal—left the country or risked imprisonment or a gruesome death at home.[7]

In 1945, when Koreans could again condemn Japan wherever they were, the issue of *what* had been illegal became trickier to harness, not that there wasn't plenty to be angry about. Immediately after Japan's surrender, the U.S. occupation government in Tokyo prepared a quick report concerning Japanese possessions in Korea, and even though the report's authors knew then that their results were incomplete, they determined that Japan controlled roughly 85 percent of all assets in the country. It is significant that, according to the report, the Japanese government and the nation's major corporations owned approximately 83 percent of this total.[8]

Especially interesting now is that many of the histories that fuel Korean resentment *today* about the Japanese era took decades to find a place for themselves in the national narrative. Most noticeable, far more crucial to this dynamic now are stolen lives, not stolen property. The well-known traumas of the former comfort women, for example, did not become the touchstone for declaring the illegality of the Japanese era—as they are today—until the 1990s when it became socially possible within Korea and within Japan for some of the surviving women to speak and demonstrate publicly about their lived past.[9]

The shifting emphasis from property theft to robbing people of their lives points to a new and wholly different kind of predicament that arose for Koreans in 1945 compounding the problems of a divided country: the dilemma of folding law into history to correct past injustices. The passage of time has only intensified this difficulty. In addition to radically different social conditions within Korea today compared to sixty years ago—let alone a hundred years ago when Japanese colonization began—one of the biggest barriers to doing anything *now* with Korean claims about the illegality of the era of Japanese rule is that imperialism has never been declared illegal. As a result, when Koreans denounce the illegality of the Japanese era today, they call into question the legality of imperialism itself in compelling ways, whether intentionally or not. Yet who would judge this charge? Would other—if not all—imperialist histories also need to be declared illegal? Would the nineteenth and twentieth centuries?

Japan's 1910 annexation of Korea met the standard operating definition of empire.[10] This included the numerous forced and forged colonial treaties, the directed assassination of Korea's leaders (including the now officially documented murder of the country's queen in 1895), the outright theft of villages and towns, and the enslavement of various parts of the population (also proven). That said, as with the Belgian Congo, British India, French Indochina, and the American Philippines, just because these events were considered "okay" in the prevailing views of the day does not mean that the history and memory of them should be settled today, as some would like to believe.

Moreover, the problem of Korea's place within the Japanese empire presented itself right away as a major hurdle for Koreans making claims against Japan. The Japanese ruled Korea for decades, creating the immediate sticking point for post-1945 Korean leaders that millions of Koreans had served in the Japanese war effort, involuntarily and not. In 1951, Washington wanted to include as many noncommunist states as possible in the San Francisco peace settlement with Japan where Tokyo's first international stance on the war and empire would emerge, yet British leaders in particular regarded South Korean desires to sit at the Allies' table absurd if not obscene. British and Commonwealth soldiers' memories of the brutality of Korean soldiers serving as prison camp guards of the Japanese Army in what was then still Burma or Malaysia powerfully informed this sentiment. As a result, the efforts of South Korean leaders to try to explain, for example, that one of their progenitor groups, the Provisional Government of the Korean Republic, had declared war on Japan in 1941 from their exile in Shanghai fell on deaf ears.[11]

It is interesting, however, that had the international community recognized the 1907 demands of a Korean legal scholar turned guerilla leader named Ho Wi things *might* have been easier for Korean claims after Japanese rule ended. Ho declared that the Righteous Army (*Uibyong*) insurgency that he and a few others led against Japan was a legitimate war of national defense according to international law.[12] If the world's so-called first-rank nations had agreed with him at the time, then at least later Koreans *might* have convincingly argued that Korea had been at war with Japan the whole time, making the Allied/ Axis distinction moot. But all this is only speculation anyway—counterfactual history—because, in 1907, no one outside Korea except Japanese officials paid any attention to Ho Wi's declaration of war, and, moreover, they threw him in jail and tortured him to death.

This particular history is more of an issue than the martyrdom of one man. Although the insurgency that Ho and his comrades led was a significant, armed anti-Japanese movement involving tens of thousands of men at its peak during 1907–1909, contrary to the wishful desires of countless later Korean narratives, it wasn't a national war of resistance against Japan. To be fair, there was no way in the 1890s or the early 1900s that Koreans could have fought such a war, as they were just then formulating the elements of a modern nation-state, something from which Chinese Nationalists (and Communists, too, for that matter) later benefited. At the outset of the twentieth century, the very idea of being Korean was on the verge of becoming possible in a country where a centuries-old aristocratic order made it not yet possible to call the population together in the country's name to fend off the Japanese.[13] But that is precisely what made Korea ripe for the picking at the time. Like Vietnam, Indonesia, Egypt, Morocco, and even China at that moment for the British, there was no nation to die for when the imperial powers colonized them.

With the exception of Ho Wi, the Righteous Army's other leaders and fighters defined what they were doing in Confucian terms of defending the virtue of the realm. Lacking the support of the Korean government, which was increasingly controlled by and working with Japan at the time, the movement failed to meet the modern legal definition of war. And, although several Koreans outside the country subsequently organized or participated in governments-in-exile that declared their own wars on Japan (including both Syngman Rhee and Kim Il Sung as well as emigrant groups such as those in Hawaii and San Francisco), unlike China in the 1930s, Korea was never officially at war with Japan *within* Korea, making its post-1945 claims about the illegality of Japan's rule all the more retroactive and all the more involved with the problem of the legality of imperialism itself. As it stands in terms of history, Japan invaded Korea, overcame occasionally fierce resistance, and stayed to rule until 1945 when ruling Japan itself became a problem.

It is no surprise, however, that the brief flash of the Righteous Army movement's history today fuels strong identifying narratives about Korean resolve and brotherhood across time and space. Visiting various well-funded national museums of Korean pride might lead you to believe that every young man—and sometimes woman—in the country took part, especially the poor ones. But that is the point. Since the end of the Japanese era, both South and North Korean governments (and particularly the South because of its failure to have substantive purge trials) have needed all Koreans to connect with the idea of the illegality of Japan's actions because it helps organize them as Koreans today.

At the Independence Memorial Hall in Chungcheong, South Korea, for example, there is a diorama on a table the size of a small school classroom. On top, hundreds of tiny figurines dressed in the now romanticized rag tag of the Righteous Army—they did not have national backing, so they did not have uniforms, and they made or stole what weapons they had—fiercely tackle heavily armed figurines dressed in Japanese Imperial Army uniforms. Here and there, Japanese toy soldiers hack off the limbs and heads of helpless Korean peasants, while Righteous Army fighters gut and skewer the menacing Japanese. Bright red nail polish makes it all livelier for the legions of children and military servicemen there on mandatory patriotic education trips.[14]

In a similar vein, Kim Hyeon-seok's 2002 film, *YMCA Baseball Team*, also feeds desires for a plucky past regardless of the details. The movie's charm and costumes make it a fairly innocuous way to waste ten dollars, as does the ever popular smile of megastar Song Gang-ho who plays the clean-up batter on Korea's first baseball team organized by YMCA missionaries in Seoul in 1905. The story is simple, but who cares, because you want the scrappy Korean team to beat the pants off the snotty Japanese. That's the kind of movie it is.

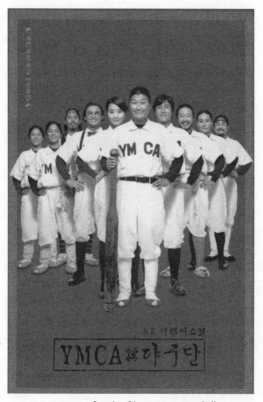

FIGURE 3.2 Poster for the film *YMCA Baseball Team*, 2002
(Myung Films Distribution)

The film finds a telling need, however, to incorporate a fiction-alized version of the most famous upper-class suicide in modern Korean history—court official Min Yonghwan's 1905 sacrifice pro-testing Japan's actions—as a plot device to set in motion the exploits of a resistance group that never existed (the "Anti-Ulsa Fifty"). Like the museum's display, the movie is part of a broad social under-standing which fans notions that the Koreans lost their country mainly because they were the underdogs. Although certainly a more pleasing story, such versions only fuel the "ruse of history" approach to the past yet block out the reckoning that still needs to take place to unravel how, for example, the high school squad of Japanese boys

FIGURE 3.3 Japanese students in Seoul playing baseball, 1908
(Takushoku University Archives)

pictured here in Seoul in 1908 got there in the first place, and the manner in which they and their children would stay.

ILLEGAL JAPAN AND THE ISLAND DISPUTE

These days, when tempers flare over fishing and natural gas rights around the islands that Japan and Korea argue about, the level of tension might suggest that the resource issue would clarify what is going on. Or, as some might say, it would finally explain the "real" reason behind regional instability. Yet, the natural resources explanation skirts the very significant issue of *how* these waters came to cause such tension in the first place, let alone how they relate to the idea of an illegal Japan. The use of natural resources around the contested islands has surfaced regularly since 1965, when South Korea and Japan established relations. Because these fall under Seoul's purview alone, and because South Koreans so readily wrap beliefs about the Japanese era around the islands on a popular level, this issue reveals itself as an unusually integral part of South Korea's narrative of illegal Japan.

First of all, given the fervor that can arise over otherwise tedious details of international relations such as fishing's exclusive economic zones (EEZs) you might think that the area's produce was the life-blood of daily consumption.

The waters are rich and full of sweet crabs, pearly squid, and prized sea bream, in addition to the lure of potential energy reserves beneath the ocean floor. Yet, unlike three hundred years ago, or even sixty, the fish drawn from these remarkably deep waters no longer *has* to feed the area's population, let alone that of either nation involved, which North Korea's profound hunger and poverty less than two hundred miles away makes painfully clear by comparison. Looked at differently, if Seoul and Tokyo were to designate this ocean area an off-limits, multinational nature preserve—a watery DMZ instead of an EEZ—their people could still survive very well. The area's produce is, instead, part of the reason that Koreans enjoy traveling to the disputed islands from their side and Japanese to the coastal area nearest to them on theirs. While singing "Dokdo is Our Land" by day, for example, Koreans return at night to restaurants on nearby Ulleungdo to enjoy feasts of the tasty local morsels.

To be sure, such an idea would outrage fisherman who would become *further* under- and unemployed, and the price of squid would go up. Yet, in daily life most South Koreans and Japanese (including fishermen) eat so much processed food and food imported from mass agribusinesses in the U.S. and China that, although the products caught here still matter to many and still have real flavor, they no longer count as sustenance foods. And while, of course, it would be good to locate new energy supplies in the area, South Koreans and Japanese will continue for the foreseeable future to stay warm, drive cars, and do their cooking with oil and gas that comes almost entirely from the Middle East. Only these countries' respective nuclear power plants offer a so-called indigenous source, which is likely to prevail unless we all go solar or commit to harvesting wind and wave motion very soon.

And here, as in many places, a little history helps explain why the national resources issue has gained so much ground at the expense of examining what is really involved. Included in the August 1945 directives that General MacArthur sent to the defeated Japanese government from his desk in the Philippines was an order grounding Japanese fishermen.[15] MacArthur wanted to ensure a smooth landing for the U.S. occupation forces—which would number 350,000 by the end of 1945—but this initial action soon developed into what was called the "MacArthur Line," a waterline boundary around Japan determining who and what could go where.

Although these limits did not compete then with questions of survival for most Japanese, in important ways MacArthur's net began to plot the new shape of post-empire Japan. SCAP Instruction 1033 followed on June 22, 1946, allowing Japanese fishermen back into broader reaches of the oceans east, south, and southwest of Japan's main islands and returned them to the waters in the west around Tsushima, which is the large island off Kyushu closest to Korea that locals call Japan's "final frontier." It also permitted them back into the waters south of Korea's southern Jeju island. At the same time, however, the order stipulated that no Japanese ships or people were allowed closer than twelve miles away from the islands that are disputed today, which were drawn then on the map as Korean territory but called "Takeshima."

The issue of who controlled the waters around Takeshima/Dokdo and what was in them, however, was clearly *not* an issue for Koreans in the years immediately following the collapse of Japanese rule. Despite the ways in which the MacArthur Line affected Korea—Japanese fishing boats would come so close to Korea that Korean and American authorities routinely seized them—there was no popular or official Korean response to MacArthur's rules. Even more revealingly, in 1948 there was no large public outcry in Korea when American Air Force planes bombed and killed as many as a few hundred Korean fishermen on and around the contested islands. The tragic incident happened because neither the U.S. military authority in Korea nor the Koreans themselves understood the details of MacArthur's fishing guidelines for Japan.

Only *after* the U.S. military withdrew almost completely from South Korea in the summer of 1949 (before it came back in force to stay for the war in 1950 and its aftermath), and only then when Syngman Rhee's claims to power at home became even shakier, did the matter of the natural resources surrounding the contested islands as well as the islands themselves take root and germinate South Korea's narrative of the illegality of Japanese rule. In June 1949, when news reached Korea that U.S. occupation authorities in Japan were expanding the MacArthur Line, Korean politicians and newspaper editors seized on it, and for the first time collectively denounced all things Japanese. In doing so they planted the idea of "illegal Japan" in popular consciousness.

That the frenzy over fishing boundaries began entirely as a domestic issue in South Korea is beyond question. The print media in wide circulation at the time (the *Chosun Ilbo* and the *Donga Ilbo*) needed something with which to sever itself from its Japanese-era roots, and politicians ranging from Syngman Rhee to members of the as-Left-as-they-could-be Tongsong-hoe political party saw in the fishing issue a way to demonstrate just how Korean they were. For everyone involved, of course, unification with North Korea was *the* issue—as it remains today—and using the Japanese era as a means to reach and manipulate public sentiment at whim proved to be an incredibly powerful tool.

Although living conditions in South Korea today could not be more different from those in 1949—South Korea was comparable at the time to the poorest nations of Africa or elsewhere in Asia, yet in 2004 it joined the world's so-called trillion dollar club—the ways Korean opinion makers condemned Japan in 1949 do not sound very different from now. In June 1949, the mainstream *Chosun Ilbo* newspaper railed against Japan's "secret, illegal" actions in Korean waters, and politicians across the board trumped up charges of Japan's renewed imperialistic militarism, which, given the conditions of Japanese industry in 1949, were far-fetched to say the least.[16]

With South Korean leaders' sudden condemnation of Japan's illegal actions, it seemed to many who were otherwise uninformed or uneducated that those in charge of the country were finally going to begin to deal with their lived needs. In 1949, millions of Korean lives remained in utter shambles because of how Japan used Korea and Koreans in its wartime attempt to control Asia and the South Pacific. Furthermore, although the Korean War would not start until June 1950, the South was already engulfed in partisan violence with *South* Korean communist insurgencies spreading throughout.[17] Once all-out war erupted, its upheavals consumed Koreans and Korean opinion, yet, during the middle of it all, Syngman Rhee realized that, once the San Francisco Treaty went into effect in April 1952, the MacArthur Line would disappear. On January 18, 1952, therefore, Rhee announced the "Rhee Line," and, not surprisingly, he put the disputed islands squarely inside his new diagram of Korean boundaries.

At the time, Rhee's attempts to unify the Korean peninsula were failing grotesquely in war, and as he campaigned throughout the summer of 1952 to continue his presidency and the war, he used the fishing issue with Japan and the disputed islands to secure his claims to control Korea. In September, he sent a South Korean naval ship to conduct "research" on the islands, and by lucky coincidence for him, U.S. Air Force planes returning from runs to North Korea again emptied unused bombs on the islands while the South Korean ship was there. This time no one died, but the incident erupted in popular opinion.

On April 20, 1953, Seoul took the opportunity to station guards on the rocks, and Japan countered with coast guard ships of its own to patrol the area. Japan's action prompted Seoul's first position paper on the matter, "The Korean Government's Refutation of the Japanese Government's Views Concerning Dokdo," which reads like a rough draft of Seoul's more current and more polished version.[18] In 1954, South Korea made more visible claims to the islands by building an unwieldy concrete lighthouse and a helicopter landing pad, and placing a permanent defense unit there. As Japanese officials scrambled around clamoring on about Korea's "illegal occupation" and demanding that the issue be taken to the International Court of Justice, Seoul issued a Dokdo

FIGURE 3.4 South Korean postage stamp, 1954
(Republic of Korea Postal Service)

postage stamp to help South Koreans celebrate their new eastern border.

LEGAL SOUTH KOREA

Many wonder today how South Koreans could continue to rally around the idea of an illegal Japan more easily than anything else except soccer. In the current South Korea—especially Seoul—of sleek cell phones, cutting-edge film and fashion, it is all too easy to forget that as recently as 1997 people still "disappeared" Latin American-style for their determination to bring an end to dictatorial politics and make South Korea a democracy. Although hard to fathom while traveling around the country today, during the sixties, seventies, and eighties, tear-gas drenched protests, armor-clad riot police, arrests, forced silences, and shattered futures patterned much of South Korean life.[19]

Therefore, when thinking historically about the country's post-Japan era, it is essential to remember that South Korea's military regimes ruled for about the same amount of time that the Japanese did, and they did so until *much more* recently. Claiming to be democratic, these dictatorial governments ruled according to the infamous 1948 National Security Law outlawing communism. Through this law, officials would defame or execute their detractors by naming them "communist" and charging them with treason. Although the law has undergone several important changes since its creation, it remains on the books. To say that South Koreans still have to unravel *this* past is an understatement. The January 2007 outcry among ruling members of South Korean society *against* disclosing the names of judges and lawyers who worked for the military regimes brought home just how far away that moment is.[20]

Compounding that, however, and vital to any analysis of South Korea's postcolonial problems with Japan is understanding that during the dictatorships you could not be arrested for being "anti-Japanese." In other words, for most of the era from 1945 until now, any issue involving Japan combined the volatile elements of unaccounted for history, individual and social memory, and cathartic release.

In 1992, Kim Young-sam won what many consider the first open presidential election in South Korea's history. Kim Dae-jung's 1997 victory confirmed the trend, and tens of thousands who had struggled with him and had suffered for so much of their lives against the dictatorships triumphed in bringing democracy to a country that had claimed to be one since 1948. President Kim—the so-called Nelson Mandela of Asia—was himself jailed numerous times and tortured under the National Security Law, and between October 2000 and October 2002 he backed a truth commission to investigate what were called "suspicious deaths" in the nation's recent history. Its report appeared quickly, as did the English translation, and, although the prose is rather dry, anyone interested in Northeast Asian history and politics as well as international human rights issues should read the case studies alone.[21]

The report is a window onto official South Korea passing judgment on its recent self, and, as such, it is by nature a top-down view that is not directly related to the history and apology problems between Korea and Japan. The way the commissioners judged their country's contemporary society, however, helps illuminate why the idea of an illegal Japan would hold such appeal across South Korean society.

Commissioners begin the report, for example, by admitting South Korea's deep structural connections to the Japanese era:

The apparatus for suppressing the people, enlarged from the colonial period through the Korean War, grew tremendously during the military regime, until no sector of society was free from its control. The KCIA (Korean Central Intelligence Agency) was synonymous with omnipotent power.[22]

Although not as clear a denunciation as some might want, this is a rather remarkable statement for current government officials to make about their own nation's immediate past, and, if anything, it is a healthy indicator of how far democracy has come in South Korea during the last decade. In Japan, by comparison, officially sponsored inquiries into Japan's responsibility for wartime atrocities continue to insist on a total break between pre and post-1945 Japan, regardless of whether this makes sense. The postwar resurrection of some of Japan's wartime leaders alone makes this more than difficult to square with people; for example, Class-A war criminal Kishi Nobusuke became the nation's prime minister from 1957 to 1960 despite having commandeered the nation's industrialization of Manchuria in the 1930s and having served as Minister of Commerce and Industry under the infamous Tojo Hideki from 1941 to 1945. (His grandson, Abe Shinzo, was the country's prime minister from 2006 to 2007 and often quoted his grandfather's advice.)

Ultimately, though, the South Korean Truth Commission adopted a temporal framework that makes South Korea's beliefs about an illegal Japan take on deeper meaning. In short, commissioners found it almost impossible to pick a point in time since South Korea's founding in 1948 that they could use as a starting date for their own record of the nation's state-sponsored violence against its citizens. The special legislation that allowed this truth commission to function in the first place stipulated that no one currently in a position of governing authority could be held accountable, yet some members of parliament and the bureaucracy today were central figures in the dictatorial regimes. Also, in many cases, their children and nephews and nieces are now in powerful positions, most noticeably Park Chung-hee's daughter, Park Geun-hye, a conservative party leader and recent presidential hopeful.

As a result, the truth commission chose August 1969 as the starting date, the date when Park Chung-hee forcibly changed the constitution to give himself a third term as "president," suggesting that the nation's laws be seen as more significant than the brutality with which the dictators came to power in terms of the state's crimes against its own. Although the commission found it awkward to set a starting date, the report makes abundantly clear that the system of rule established through the National Security Law, which operated for more than forty years *after* the Japanese era ended, not only tolerated state crimes but governed through them. As the head commissioner stated matter-of-factly, these governments ruled "behind the guise of temporary legality."[23]

South Korea's official charade worked because the gashes of the Japanese era remained untreated—thousands of forcibly conscripted laborers, for example, remained abandoned and impoverished in places as distant as Sakhalin Island—on top of which there had been no purge trials. Had there been, of course, leaders such as Park Chung-hee and Chun Doo-hwan, among others, would likely have been in jail or hanged before the Korean War began.[24] The ploys of the military government compounded over the years in odd ways into common sense. During the widespread demonstrations in 1965 against Park Chung-hee's decision to establish normalized ties with Tokyo, protest signs read, "Stop New Colonialism!!" and "Don't Sell Us Out Again!!" Ironically, however, others simultaneously decried Park's decision to rescind South Korea's "Peace Line"—as the "Rhee Line" had become popularly known—in favor of a new fisheries agreement with Tokyo, because, as the logic ran, the Japanese would only use the new boundaries to resume their one-sided illegal behavior.

Throughout, however, many South Koreans raised more than eyebrows at the military regime's strategy of illegal Japan as foil to the legal dictators at home, with writers and artists routinely risking their lives in the tangible protest of poetry, painting, theater, and dance. In 1967, one of the country's bleaker novelists, Choi In-hoon, published a short story titled "The Voice of the Governor General," in which an unnamed voice on the radio welcomes himself back to rule Korea after an absence of "more than twenty years."[25] The voice revels that the opportunity now exists "to regain lost territory, to

FIGURE 3.5 Protest in Seoul against normalization
with Japan, 1965 (*Donga Ilbo*)

repossess the Peninsula, (which) is the dream of the Empire." The
moment in real life came on the heels of Park's signing the so-called
normalization treaty with Japan, and the "empire" could either be
the former Japanese empire or Park's rule or a combination of both,
as Park had served officially for the Japanese colonial government.
Although censorship was a defining feature of Park's command, the
writer trumped his censors because he never named the voice, nor
did he identify the speaker as Korean (though it clearly is Park). Korean history and social memory would only agree with the story's
purported condemnation of Japanese rule.

The idea of an illegal Japan exploded in the 1990s on a transnational scale, adding much broader dimensions to Korea's domestic narrative. The 1989 death of Japanese wartime emperor Hirohito coincided with widespread democratization trends in South Korea, making it possible to tell old histories to new audiences in public. The comfort women of the Japanese military, forcibly conscripted soldiers, and enslaved laborers found increasing reception for their stories, all of which, simply by existing, belied Japan's popular modern myths about its so-called war of liberation in Asia in the 1930s and 1940s.

All the survivors of Japan's history of violence share wretched stories of abuse and deprivation, yet during the 1990s the comfort women became synonymous with illegal Japan. Reasons for their international recognition over that of others range from the ongoing instances of rape camps in other conflicts around the world to the disturbing, prurient gaze with which some view these now eighty- and ninety-year-old women. Since the comfort women's story broke internationally in 1991, countless newspaper articles, feature stories, doctoral dissertations, history books, novels, testimonials, songs, and films in numerous languages have come to tell the women's experience with painful similarity: of the up to two hundred thousand women and girls who were part of Japan's state-organized system of sexual servitude, most were kidnapped or tricked into their involvement.[26] The largest number were Korean, and many others were Chinese, Taiwanese, Filipino, Indonesian, and Dutch. In 2006, the global movement to stop violence against women and girls known as "V-Day," an offshoot of American playwright Eve Ensler's phenomenon, *The Vagina Monologues*, made the surviving women its "spotlight" group for the year, speaking to the impact their history continues to have, given that the "women of Iraq" held the position in 2005.[27]

In January 2007, members of the U.S. Congress began considering a resolution to call on Japan to accept responsibility and atone for this particular outrage, and hearings were held in mid-February

What does this DO?

during which three former comfort women testified.[28] Unlike previous attempts to pass similar resolutions, this one succeeded on
July 30, 2007, in no small part because the Japanese government's
highly paid Washington lobbyists failed to do their routine, pricey
damage control. Midway in the procedures, Prime Minister Abe declared that the Americans did not know "the facts" and denied that
the Japanese government "coerced" the women into the system. The
pattern of Abe and his supporters' behavior shocked many around
the world and significantly compounded the image of illegal Japan
as far as this history was concerned. A *New York Times* editorial point-
edly demanded, "What part of 'Japanese Army sex slaves' does Japan's prime minister have so much trouble understanding and
apologizing for?"[29]

A grass-roots South Korean women's organization, The Korean
Council for Women Drafted into Sexual Slavery, is largely responsible for the world knowing about the comfort women and their
horrible history.[30] Beginning in the late 1980s, its organizers began
working with survivors and encouraged them to come forward with
their stories as the most productive way to reclaim their dignity. Of
equal significance, they also began collaborating with Japanese wom-
en's groups sympathetic to their cause.[31] In August 1991, former
South Korean comfort woman Kim Hak-soon made her story public, and an international media frenzy erupted. It is telling that human rights groups such as Amnesty International began to shift
their efforts away from members of South Korea's suppressed democracy movement onto the women. The horror of these particular
victims' stories seemed all the worse because they were now elderly,
not very well educated, and had led overwhelmingly marginal lives
since Japan's defeat in 1945.

Beginning with the January 18, 1992, declaration of "remorse" by
Japanese Prime Minister Miyazawa Kiichi for Japan's use of comfort women during the war, most of Tokyo's succeeding prime min-
isters and countless government officials repeated and expanded on
these words; the 1993 statement of ruling party parliamentarian
Kono Yohei became the benchmark:

It is apparent that there existed a great number of comfort women. Comfort stations were operated in response to the request of the military authorities of the day. The then Japanese military was, directly or indirectly, involved in the establishment and management of the comfort stations and the transfer of comfort women. The recruitment of the comfort women was conducted mainly by private recruiters who acted in response to the request of the military. The Government study has revealed that in many cases they were recruited against their own will, through coaxing coercion, etc., and that, at times, administrative/military personnel directly took part in the recruitments. They lived in misery at comfort stations under a coercive atmosphere. As to the origin of those comfort women who were transferred to the war areas, excluding those from Japan, those from the Korean Peninsula accounted for a large part. The Korean Peninsula was under Japanese rule in those days, and their recruitment, transfer, control, etc., were conducted generally against their will, through coaxing, coercion, etc.[32]

Despite such statements, however, the Japanese government failed to reach consensus that the state should take responsibility for this history and refused to authorize the individual apology and reparations that most of the surviving women *still* seek.

Frustrated by their own government, some Japanese officials and sympathetic citizens established "The Asian Women's Fund," offering what sponsors and detractors alike called "a quasi-official apology" and a small cash payment from money collected through private donations. Attacked from all sides as either whitewash or treachery, the Fund disbanded in 2007 not in the least because "compassion fatigue," to use media critic Susan Moeller's term, had begun to sink in years earlier even among concerned Japanese.[33] In other words, the media so saturated its own market that people started turning away without listening anymore.

From one perspective, the Japanese government long maneuvered within the bounds of apology politics concerning the comfort women, officially acknowledging no more than various pressures made incumbent upon it. As important, however, and differing significantly from the island or Yasukuni Shrine disputes, the South Korean government does not regularly rely on the comfort women's history as a stumbling block in its official relations with Tokyo. The historical combination of the place of women in Korean society during the centuries leading up to Japan's colonization and the impoverished backgrounds from which most came placed these survivors of Japan's violence in a position of double jeopardy. The women who lived through the experience and managed to return to Korea risked enormous social prejudice at home should their story become known.[34] Regardless that they were forced to have sex with up to as many as forty men a day, regardless that they were beaten for protesting, in a society with strong Confucian overtones that privilege chastity, survivors were without a doubt impure as a result of their history. Moreover, for the most part, Japanese men had "spoiled" them, compounding modern nationalized hatreds on top of older beliefs. For decades after their return, the women led quiet, poor, and largely hidden lives until they became the cause célèbre of the international illegal Japan trend of the 1990s, raising all sorts of disturbing questions about what can happen to history's victims when their stories become politicized.

Most revealing in this regard, in 1998, even South Korea's most famous champion of human rights, Kim Dae-jung, failed the women while he was president, revealing the depth of intermingled factors involved. In an interview with Japan's leading current affairs journal, President Kim said that although the Japanese government was responsible for compensating victims, he would personally refrain from lodging a protest at the UN on the living survivors' behalf. He said, "Although Japan's 'comfort women' incident was indeed horrendous, what Germany did to Jews was even worse. The German people, however, have recognized this fact and educate their children accordingly."[35] As South Korea's head of state, Kim Dae-jung was the only person at the time in a position that could substantively challenge Japan's official statements about "the past," including whether Tokyo would pay attention to what the women wanted. Kim tailored his words according to the accepted discourse on apology, maintaining the question, "Why can't Japan be more like Germany?" while cheapening his own citizens' claims to their dignity.

As famous as the survivors of the comfort system may have become, however, their efforts only multiplied the difficulties they face in securing their place in modern Japanese history. More important, the Japanese government did not suddenly become involved just because some old women started appearing on television telling horrible stories. Throughout the 1990s, survivors and their Japanese, Korean, and Chinese supporters began a series of lawsuits in Japanese courts seeking apology and reparations for their individual pasts from the Japanese government. Despite numerous victories in lower and regional courts, Japan's higher courts (including the Supreme Court) routinely overturned judgments favorable to the victims. Many continue to sue, however, for the simple reason that they want to know before they die that their existence mattered.[36]

The lawsuits extended eastward across the Pacific as well. Emboldened by Jewish groups suing Germany in U.S. courts, in July 1999, Asian-American and Canadian groups successfully lobbied for a California state law that would allow *any* victim of forced labor in the Second World War—Koreans, Chinese, or American POWs, for example—to make claims in California courts against those responsible.[37] The law remains in force until 2010, and more than thirty cases against sixty Japanese corporations were filed in its first two years alone, further internationalizing the idea of an illegal Japan.

Ratcheting things up a notch, in September 2000 lawyers working on behalf of former South Korean comfort woman, Hwang Geum Joo, and others, became one of two suits filed in U.S. courts against the Japanese government.[38] By 2005, however, a Washington, D.C., circuit court on remand from the U.S. Supreme Court defeated the case because the judges ruled it was a "nonjusticiable political question" and "inimical to the foreign policy interests of the United States," meaning that, in their opinion, the case had no business being in the courts, let alone U.S. courts.[39] Put differently, the judges said, fight it out back home.

The question of who defines law emerged in unusual ways. Most notable was when a different kind of international court convened in

Tokyo in December 2000 to try the comfort women's history. The Korean Council and the Japanese feminist group, Violence Against Women in War-Network Japan, sponsored the Women's International War Crimes Tribunal on Japan's Military Sexual Slavery. The two main groups worked with numerous other women's groups from the Philippines, Japan, China, and Indonesia, and their efforts' gathered about sixty surviving comfort women from throughout the Asia-Pacific region and attracted more than a thousand supporters to a rented auditorium in central Tokyo where they put the Japanese government on trial for its history of state-sponsored violence.

Naysayers belittled the event as a "mock trial" with no legal authority, yet organizers heralded it as a "people's court" and secured the services of very real international judges such as Gabriella Kirk MacDonald, president of the Yugoslavia War Crimes Tribunal, and Carmen Maria Argibay, president of the International Women's Association of Judges. After listening to the women's testimony and considering lawyers' arguments, the tribunal judged the then already dead Emperor Hirohito guilty of war crimes and crimes against humanity and urged that the matter be forwarded to the International Court of Justice in The Hague. Although conceptually awkward and not a final resolution, the survivors didn't care. They danced with their arms in the air, hugged each other, hugged spectators, and several rushed the podium to bow before the judges: their story mattered.

Every now and then during the tribunal, when words failed one of the women, she would lift her shirt to reveal where a breast had been lopped off by an angry soldier, and another would point to a long scarred gash on her stomach where, more than half a century earlier, a Japanese soldier or doctor had sliced her open to remove an unborn child. One woman had no tongue; a Japanese man cut it out for trying to resist him. She spoke with her arms and eyes. To the women who felt safe telling their stories and to those in the audience, it did not seem to matter whether the tribunal had the authority to pass "real" judgment.

The fundamental question remains, then, of why these women can move the world so readily to agree with the idea of an illegal Japan, and yet make no legal headway for themselves. For the South Korean women who survived sexual slavery, as well as for the men who survived their labor in Japanese coal mines and munitions factories, the problem lies in the terms of South Korea and Japan's 1965 Treaty on Basic Relations. Like the 1951 San Francisco Treaty ending war between Japan and the Allies from which it derives, it declares that all issues involving compensation and reparations claims are settled by the treaty, disavowing the possibility of future claims. Since then, all judicial decisions in Japan and the United States concerning the comfort women have upheld this principle at the highest level, making the results, by definition, at least democratically achieved.

In Korea, in 1965, part of the reason that demonstrators charged Park Chung-hee with "selling the country away again" when he signed the treaty with Japan was that the agreement closed the books on Korean reparations claims against Japan. How was this different, some wondered, from 1910, when Korea's notorious prime minister, Yi Wanyong, signed over Korean sovereignty to Japan? In 1965, some South Korean diplomats even went so far as to agree with Japan that, by granting South Korea Japanese "assistance money," North Korea's claims would be settled as well.

As Park Chung-hee's massive domestic industrialization schemes followed, activists railed that Park and his cronies must be reaping huge profits by accepting the terms of the agreement at the expense of letting other Koreans (who, unlike Park, suffered at the hands of the Japanese) receive compensation or make claims against Japan. Yet they could not prove it until 2005, when the South Korean government's declassification of thousands of documents related to the 1965 treaty confirmed their suspicions.[40] Although the Japanese government has yet to comply fully for its side, the South Korean records alone make clear that Park as well as *still* politically active men such as Kim Jong-pil took Japan's money and more in exchange for any future Koreans to make claims. The long-known figure of $600 million now includes at least an additional $800 million at a time when South Korea's per

FIGURE 3.6 "Let's Move Ahead with Economic Development" (*Hankyoreh*)

capita income was roughly $100. South Korean cartoonist, Jang Bong-jun, perfectly captured the scenario in his drawing of a Japanese official tossing money at Park and Kim as their hapless countrymen look on.

The declassification project for 1965 documents is part of a broader South Korean governmental initiative to "research collaborationist activities" by ferreting out those Koreans who benefited unjustly from their connection with Japan's rule of the country. But with a gap of more than sixty years, the endeavor does not even remotely resemble holding purge trials on the scene or even convening a truth commission, since most of the main offenders are dead. A skeptic might think of it as doing "Korean history," the non-"ruse" kind, that is. Thus far, conclusions are fairly limited, with results including the literature faculty of Seoul National University apologizing in August 2002 for the department's colonial-era origins and the publication in August 2005 of a list of 3,090 known collaborators (out of Korea's population of 25 million at the time), making the whole process appear partial at best. Activists remain undaunted, with a recent protest song featuring the unusual refrain of "Koreans, get out and learn your history!!"

AND THEN

"They would appear to be throwing some sort of fruit," the BBC reporter Chris Gunness announced over a World Service broadcast from Busan in mid-December 2002. "Yes, yes, they are definitely throwing apples, let me go see what this is all about." In Korean, the words for "apple" and "apology" sound the same (*sagwa*), and, during the 2002–2003 winter protest movement against the ongoing presence of the U.S. military in South Korea, demonstrators' demands for apologies from the U.S. for civilian deaths caused by American soldiers reached a fever pitch. In at least one demonstration in Busan, protestors hurled apples around to make their point.

During these months, I had the unusual and wholly unrelated pleasure of helping a very thoughtful senior South Korean official practice his English. Once a week, we would sit in his office in the Central Government Building in Seoul, adjacent to the palace grounds that paved over the old Japanese administration complex and across the street from the increasingly fortressed American Embassy. He knew I studied Japanese history and took delight in using the issue of apology between Korea and Japan to practice his conversational skills. One evening, with the sounds of protestors in front of the nearby U.S. Embassy too loud too ignore, I asked him when the government of South Korea would ask the United States to apologize. He leaned back into his big, black leather chair, folded his hands across his chest, and smiled. "We are only Korea. We can only ask Japan."

Chapter Four

History Out of Bounds

On Saturday evening, December 14, 2002, about fifty thousand South Koreans gathered for a demonstration in downtown Seoul's City Hall plaza. Scores of photographers and TV cameramen stood on top of the surrounding office buildings and hotels ready to capture images of the crowd exploding into the kind of violence that made South Korea internationally famous in the 1980s. Instead of Molotov cocktails, however, pictures show only thousands of glittering little flames burning from candles in paper cups that the protestors held. The cups were covered with the school photos of two teenage girls who had been run over by a fifty–ton U.S. Army mine-removal vehicle as they walked along a country road to a friend's birthday party the previous June.

With lights spelling out "Season's Greetings" in English sparkling around the square, the tens of thousands of demonstrators—including countless families with small children—demanded an apology from Washington for the girls' deaths. They also called for revisions to South Korea's security agreement with the United States as they sang the year's most popular carol: "Fucking USA." The singer leading

FIGURE 4.1 City Hall, Seoul, December 2002 (*Korea Herald*)

the crowd was kind of a tuneful Bob Dylan, and his backup group consisted of three women in their late thirties to early forties, dressed in fashionable, activist duffle-coat style, doing a low-key version of the Rockettes' kick-turn line dance. At one point massive American flags covered the crowd, and these were eventually ripped apart but not burned.

About three weeks earlier, a U.S. military court had convened in Seoul and determined that the road accident was "unavoidable," acquitting the two soldiers who were driving the armored car. The soldiers were flown out of Korea immediately, and what had been sporadic demonstrations since June's tragedy spread overnight into a nationwide, anti-American movement, gaining rapid momentum everywhere from Catholic convents to elementary schools, where homework assignments encouraged children to express their confusion and anger over the girls' deaths and the U.S. military tribunal's judgment of the soldiers' innocence.

Almost doubly tragic for the girls' families, South Korea's 2002 presidential campaign was in full swing when this national frustra-

FIGURE 4.2 Korean girls killed in June 2002 (From a protest leaflet)

tion erupted, and none of the candidates could resist becoming involved. By the time of the December 20 election, each of the main
contenders had either visited the families' homes to pay his respects,
or attended memorial services or candlelight vigils, and all had used
the girls' story in stump speeches.

Immediately after the movement began, however, it was clear that
the protestors' demands for a stronger South Korean stance vis-à-vis
the United States would buoy the chances of the liberal/populist
candidate Roh Moo-hyun. The man many had considered the
front-runner before the demonstrations expanded, Lee Hoi-chang,
quickly seemed too cozy with Washington. As Lee desperately tried
to recast his image, unusual events began to happen, including President George Bush's November 27 condolences for the girls' deaths
issued through the then American ambassador to Seoul, Thomas
Hubbard.[1] Although no public evidence exists to suggest an ulterior
motive on Washington's part, many South Koreans instantly leapt on
Bush's timing ("Why not last June?" became one protest chant) and
upped the ante, saying nothing less would suffice than George Bush
himself coming to Seoul to deliver a "direct apology."[2]

South Korea's presidential candidates understood the depth of
the country's mood and quickly latched onto the language of "direct
apology." Together they sensed that the winner of the 2002 election
would need to articulate this emotion as national policy because
the protestors on the streets were not just student activists: they
were noticeably middle-class and middle-aged men and women with

FIGURE 4.3 Anti-Bush leaflet demanding a "direct apology"

families and mortgages who were fed up with the accidental and
purposeful violence against civilians that American soldiers stationed in South Korea so routinely commit. Therefore, in addition
to drawing attention to the lived reality of America's military presence in South Korea—a long-standing issue—this moment also shed
light on why Seoul's official demands for more public apologies
from Japan have increased during recent years.

In South Korea, intrinsic to the nation's democratization process
has been a widening determination to gain popular control over the
apologies that the country's leaders have long performed in hand-
shakes and bows behind closed doors. It is noteworthy that this
phenomenon has encouraged a related South Korean movement
with Vietnam to apologize for Seoul's sending three hundred thousand troops to assist in the American war there.[3] In South Korea, any
part of *this* history—let alone atonement for it—was so taboo until
recently that even Francis Ford Coppola's 1979 film, *Apocalypse Now*,
could only be shown in Korean theaters after its 2001 re-release.

Unfortunately for the dead girls' parents, Seoul finds that it is not
(yet?) in South Korea's national interests to demand official apologies from the United States, unlike Japan. Although the presidential
candidates could clamor along with protestors for "direct" words and
action from Washington, South Korea's then president Kim
Dae-jung (who was ineligible for another term and free to say what-

100   HISTORY OUT OF BOUNDS

ever he wanted to at the time) calmly received the U.S. ambassador in his office to accept the American president's sentiments, underscoring the issue of relative power in political apology.

NO GUN RI

South Korean demands for a "direct apology" from the United States in December 2002 stemmed from more than just the awful end to the young lives of Mi-sun and Hyo-soon. These deaths themselves compounded a long list of violent incidents involving American soldiers and Korean civilians in South Korea, which poster-sized photographs of mutilated bodies made plain for all to see throughout Seoul's parks and on its subway walls.[4] Almost entirely underappreciated in the international coverage of the moment and yet deeply mixed into it was Korean social awareness of a different American declaration of regret for a different tragedy that had come just about two years earlier: President Bill Clinton's January 2001 statement concerning the deaths of Korean civilians killed by American soldiers in the Korean village of No Gun Ri in July 1950.

Similar to how Korea's recent protests against Japan over the islands between them seemed to collapse the nation's entire postcolonial history of rancor into one moment, South Korea's 2002–2003 mass demonstrations against the United States funneled the bitter emotions stemming from America's fifty-plus-year military presence there into one event. And during these anti-American protests, South Koreans made absolutely clear that they wanted more amends for the civilian deaths that U.S. soldiers continue to cause than what they got in 2001, when Bill Clinton told Kim Dae-jung, "On behalf of the United States of America, I deeply regret that Korean civilians lost their lives at No Gun Ri in late July, 1950."[5]

Clinton's pronouncement as well as the terms of the much longer and simultaneously issued "Statement of Mutual Understanding between the United States and the Republic of Korea on the No Gun Ri Investigations" made clear that there would be no formal American apology for the Korean deaths. Like Washington's stance on the events at My Lai in Vietnam in 1968, the American troops involved in the killings in Korea in 1950 were described as "young, under-trained, under-equipped and new to combat" as well as "legitimately fearful" of the enemy, meaning that in the end no one would be held responsible for what had happened.

Therefore, although not entirely causal, two years later when President Bush issued his "regrets" for the deaths of the two schoolgirls, South Koreans wasted no time in saying, "No. We want an *apology*," which also meant, "No. Someone must take responsibility." When Koreans demanded George Bush's appearance in Seoul to deliver America's apology, they were mirroring similar demands that call for the Japanese emperor to come to Korea to atone for Japan's past.[6]

Along with Clinton's spoken words, the "Statement of Mutual Understanding" appeared in January 2001 at the end of a sixteen-month Pentagon review process. It sought "to examine the facts and circumstances surrounding the events" that occurred under a railroad track bridge in the village of No Gun Ri in central South Korea during the early days of the Korean War in July 1950 when as many as several hundred people died.[7]

The American government's sudden interest in this history was a matter of damage control, pure and simple. For decades, historians and survivors of No Gun Ri had discussed the incident—as well as numerous others like it—drawing little if any response. In Seoul's freer political climate of the 1990s, however, some survivors petitioned the U.S. Embassy there to respond to their claims, and in 1997 one group filed for compensation with the South Korean government. In 1998, a South Korean journalist then with the Associated Press, Choe Sang-hun, chronicled survivors' efforts in Korean papers, and then, finally, on September 29, 1999, the Associated Press ran an article that was picked up worldwide as the "shocking" story of an American "massacre" of Korean civilians at No Gun Ri. The following morning, U.S. Secretary of Defense William Cohen charged Secretary of the Army Louis Caldera with conducting an investigation, as if it were news to everyone in Washington.

Lest any American may have worried that the U.S. government was embarking on a lengthy process of taxpayer-sponsored self-examination to give voice to the claims of some previously unheard of foreigners, Cohen could not have been clearer about why the Pentagon wanted to review this particular past. On September 30, 1999, he wrote Caldera: "This review is important to the active and retired members of our armed forces, the confidence of the American people in the finest armed forces around the world, and our relationship with the people of the Republic of Korea."[8]

Two weeks later Cohen sent Caldera a second letter, however, revealing that neither of them had yet fully grasped the stakes involved. The note began with Cohen's description of a recent telephone conversation with South Korean Minister of Defense Cho Song-tae who "made clear that the allegations of civilian deaths at No Gun Ri have *enormous* historical, political, and emotional importance for his government and the people of the Republic of Korea."[9] It appears that Minister Cho may have come as close as he could to demanding U.S. action, yet regardless of the level of tension involved, Cohen emphasized to Caldera that "we need to ensure that no relevant information is overlooked and that the ROK government has complete confidence that the whole story has been told. . . . [T]he Army is responsible for determining the full scope of the facts."

Most apparent from all this is that even before the U.S. Army chose people to conduct the review, the Pentagon had determined the shape of the final product.[10] Cohen mandated that the review board would affirm the justness of the American military's cause across time, which does not always have to do with what actually happened and which is what some might consider history. Most significant, the authors of America's official narrative of No Gun Ri would necessarily have to circumscribe their findings in light of the marred faces of the incident's survivors appearing at the time around the world on television and in newspapers, telling their lived nightmare of being trapped with fellow villagers under a small bridge for several days without food or water as American soldiers fired on them if they tried to move and, in some cases, even if they didn't.

It is no surprise that the Korean victims' version of what had happened to them would not be considered *as* trustworthy a source of evidence as the American perpetrators' side of the story. Although Washington would emphasize that the "highest levels of ROK and U.S. bilateral co-operation" enabled the review, in place after place in the Pentagon's report and in the "Statement's" summarized findings deep differences clearly remained along the line of "they say/we say." In such cases, the American reviewers invariably determined that the evidence "could not be confirmed." In answer to the question of how many Koreans died, the "Statement" explains: "The Koreans have reported an unverified number of 248 Korean civilians killed, injured, or missing while the testimony of U.S. veterans supports lower numbers." In the conclusion the review board maintains, "The U.S. Team believes the number to be lower than the Korean claim."[11] Was the number 30? Was it 200? How did the civilians die? The "Statement" is at its most critical of American action on this point and allows that the review team could "not exclude the possibility that U.S. or Allied aircraft might have hit civilians."[12]

Although the American veterans' testimony generated as many inconsistencies as the Korean victims' recollections, the Army reviewers followed Cohen's charge, and their word choice and writing style consistently made the U.S. soldiers' explanation of what happened at No Gun Ri appear more credible. In other words, the language of the Pentagon authors neutralized the underlying horror that their own report confirmed: U.S. troops fired on and killed many unarmed and terrified Korean adults and children. Ultimately, the "Statement" reads as "us versus them," defining the essence of a national narrative approach to history and indicative of why such methods—indeed, such "ruses"—fuel the politics of blame rather than any learning from the past. When the review was released, it was denounced so fast and furiously that President Clinton had to spend the last days of his presidency defending it and amplifying his own statements: "We are *profoundly* sorry."[13]

When Clinton first offered his regrets, he announced that in lieu of compensation payments the "United States [would] construct [a memorial] to these and all other innocent Korean civilians killed during the war [to] bring a measure of solace and closure."[14] The American government also would sponsor a "commemorative scholarship fund . . . [to] serve as a living tribute to their memory." By the end of September 2006, however, the $4 million dollar budget expired with only a portion spent on design plans, because Washington refused to grant the survivors' wish that the monument mention their history alone and not be a generalized tribute to all the civilian casualties of the war.[15] Moreover, the survivors wanted the monument to inscribe who fired the shots.

Millions of Korean civilians died during the Korean War, and clearly the American government wants to protect itself from a spiraling series of demands. This raises the question, though, of how anyone could believe that what many would call the practical approach would solve anything given that it demonstrates only that the most powerful nation in world history, for fear of lawsuits, cannot even acknowledge what happened to some unfortunate people more than half a century ago.

The South Korean government successfully lobbied the United States to prolong the fund for one more year, yet during the extension period, instead of pushing Washington to meet survivors' demands, it embarked on its own form of damage control. The "Statement" was, after all, a "Statement of *Mutual* Understanding," meaning that it was as much Seoul's as it was Washington's. South Korean officials knew that should the fund disappear without anything to show for it there could be more media attention on the victims, which might encourage more criticism of the nature of South Korea's relationship with the United States. These were not new problems, yet North Korea's October 2006 nuclear test was exacerbating them at the time.

An interesting note, however, is that as early as June 2004 South Korean officials anticipated that the pragmatic approach to which they and their American counterparts had agreed might not satisfy the desires of those who wanted to record the story in a way that was meaningful to them. As such, in Seoul's own attempt to reign in future disruptions to the nation's official relations with the United States—such as large anti-American demonstrations—the South Korean government passed a special law allocating national funds for a commemorative park that would include the kind of monument survivors wanted. Set for completion in 2009, it would seem, therefore, that the so-called pragmatic approach to narrating the story of American soldiers killing Korean civilians means that the South Korean government must frame such histories on its own out of necessity, and its citizens must pay the bill, all of which would make seemingly implausible ideas such as the U.S. government simply telling the truth appear a little more sensible.

COLLATERAL DAMAGE

Tucked into Washington's "Statement of Mutual Understanding" about No Gun Ri is a sentence that some might consider no more than a throwaway line: "Civilian casualties are, without exception, the most tragic of the unintended consequences of conflict."[16] These words, however, run so afoul of America's known record of targeting civilians during the nation's wars in Asia during and since 1945 (and before, if you go back to the Philippines in 1898 or Hawai'i in 1893 or Korea in 1871) that they wind up doing the opposite of simply padding out a bureaucratic document. Instead, they draw attention to one of America's most enduring problems in Asia and one that remains at the heart of the No Gun Ri controversy: confronting the history of killing noncombatants.[17]

Some might want to wish away the whole problem of civilian deaths, which the euphemism so coldly defines as "collateral damage" that cannot be avoided. Such relativism, however, does not calm the lived events for those involved. More fundamental in the American context, it fails to recognize America's unusual twentieth-century (and now twenty-first-century) position of having a demonstrated history of having killed hundreds of thousands of noncombatants during various wars (according to the *most* conservative estimates) while continuing to maintain huge troop presences throughout the world—especially in Asia—that cause civilian deaths unintentionally or intentionally even when no declared war is going on.

South Korean society's conflation of the two girls' deaths in 2002 with earlier histories of deaths caused by American soldiers suggests that this tense reality may have become so intractable in places where people have long lived alongside American troops that even distinctions of war and peace may no longer be useful. In other words, wartime pasts now blend into a present still surrounded by American troops. The expanding impetus for apology and reparations for history has only made things more difficult.

That the U.S. government created and perpetuates its own problems is not surprising. Without question, America's napalm-infused firebombing of Tokyo in March 1945 is elemental to its uncomfortable twentieth-century record of killing civilians, as is its decimation of Pyongyang, Hue, and eastern Cambodia. Sadly, there are many more such examples. On a different level, however, the nation's regressive refusal to deal with the human costs of nuclear warfare has even more dogmatically shaped and sustained America's narrative of denial.[18] It is ironic that the problem of apologetic history and political apology lies at its center and arguably at the core of America's post-1945 national story writ large.

One of the simplest ways to understand how nuclear weapons fit into America's problems with confronting civilian casualties is by considering Washington's control of information concerning Hiroshima and Nagasaki in the immediate wake of their destruction. The blatant contradiction, for example, between America's orders for Japan to eliminate all vestiges of the country's wartime thought-control system with its own command to cordon off southern Japan to reporting of any kind could not have been starker.

As soon as the war ended, American authorities and, more important, many Japanese began to address the so-called valley of darkness into which Japan's notorious thought police (the *kempeitai*) as well as their milder counterparts at the Ministry of Education had led society through their wartime censorship policies.[19] Collective efforts to remake Japan into a place that would encourage free speech defined much early postwar rhetoric and policy. At this very same juncture, however, U.S. officials set in motion a policy of total knowledge control about Hiroshima and Nagasaki, barring news reports, photographs, and, perhaps most disturbing, any public discussion of medical information.

Right away this is revealing, not in the least because the combined number of noncombatant deaths that America caused across the rest of Japan was higher than those in Hiroshima and Nagasaki, and these were not censored. In other words, from the start it was not so much the issue of civilian deaths per se that American authorities wanted to control but rather these deaths in particular.

The most serious rift in the restrictions concerning Hiroshima and Nagasaki occurred as General MacArthur was in the process of issuing them, when the combined response to the breach by the U.S. government and the U.S. media set in motion the pattern of denial that has existed and gained strength to this day. In his 1983 memoir, *Shadow of Hiroshima*, the Australian reporter Wilfred Burchett claims that he didn't know Hiroshima was out of bounds and traveled there in early September 1945, acting, as he said, in "obedience to the most fundamental and categorical imperative of journalism: Get to the spot as soon as you can, preferably ahead of your colleagues, and faithfully report back to your readers what you have seen and felt."[20]

Whether Burchett knew that Hiroshima was off-limits does not really matter in terms of history, because he went, wrote about what he saw, and, on September 5, 1945, the London *Daily Express* published his highly charged account on its front page under the headline: "The Atomic Plague."[21]

The article marked the first disclosure about what would come to be known as radiation sickness.[22] As such, it was also the first indication to the world beyond Japan that people could become ill or die from this weapon—and not just be blown up—making Burchett's notice of blast survivors covered with spots and with hair missing in clumps and blood coming out of their mouths a direct threat to how Washington wanted to portray its victory. The article's opening sentence alone laid waste to the American triumphalism that was already declaring the planet's bright future thanks to the new weapon: "In Hiroshima, thirty days after the first atomic bomb destroyed the city and shook the world, people are still dying, mysteriously and horribly—people who were uninjured in the cataclysm from an unknown something which I can only describe as the atomic plague."[23]

Official American repudiation of Burchett's account came swiftly from voices as seemingly different as military leaders to journalists and university presidents. Simply put, as the historian Mark Selden explains, the article "forced damage control measures . . . to reaffirm an official narrative that downplayed civilian casualties, flatly denied reports of deadly radiation and its lingering effects, and accused the reporter of falling for Japanese propaganda."[24] In light of today's embedded reporting practices in Iraq and Afghanistan, seeing how a radically different depiction of events erased Burchett's revelations revives questions about the substance of precisely what Americans would come to know as the history of Hiroshima, as well as of the nation's global preeminence that followed.

To begin with, in his memoirs Burchett describes his astonishing twenty-hour train ride from Tokyo to Hiroshima on September 2. The date matters because, on that morning, every other foreign reporter in Japan dutifully assembled aboard the USS *Missouri* in Tokyo Bay to watch and record the big history of Japanese delegates signing surrender papers with General MacArthur.

FIGURE 4.5 Carl Mydans's famous photograph of the surrender ceremony
aboard the USS *Missouri*, September 1945 (*Life*)

Meanwhile, Burchett caught the 6:00 AM train south jammed
with little histories:

> The train was overflowing with freshly demobilized troops and
> officers. The officers still wore their long swords with *samurai*
> daggers tucked into their belts.... After the first five or six
> hours, my fellow platform-swingers, ruddy of face, bleary of eyes
> and glowing with *saki*, started dropping off at the various
> stops.... No salutes, I noted, for officers who got off at the
> same stops, no bows, no signs of recognition even.... The hos-
> tility was total. An American in priest's clothes whom I ap-
> proached with exuberance, not entirely due to *saki*, warned me
> in guarded language that the situation was very tense. Then I
> noticed that he had an armed escort and was very nervous. He
> said that a smile or handshake would be taken as gloating over
> the surrender.[25]

Arriving at 2:00 AM the following day, Japanese police threw Burchett into a makeshift jail until the sun rose, when he was able to

FIGURE 4.6 Hiroshima, August 1945
(United States Army Archives)

display a letter of introduction from a Japanese reporter in Tokyo to a colleague in Hiroshima. The meeting took place, and Burchett and a Japanese journalist named Nakamura walked as best they could through "the flattened rubble of 68,000 buildings."

Surviving violent stares and moves to lynch him, Burchett and Nakamura made their way to the Hiroshima Communications Hospital among others, where Burchett had one of the first encounters that a *non*-victim would have with the city's living nightmare:

> In these hospitals, I discovered people who, when the bomb fell suffered absolutely no injuries, but now are dying from the after effects. For no apparent reason, their health began to fail. They lost appetite. Their hair fell out. Bluish spots appeared on their

bodies. And then bleeding from the ears, nose, and mouth. At first, the doctors told me, they thought these were the symptoms of general debility. They gave their patients Vitamin A injections. The results were horrible. The flesh started rotting away from the hole caused by the injection of the needle. And in every case the patient died.[26]

Burchett's account caused a worldwide sensation that was comparatively muted in the United States, which makes sense, however, given that many Americans were still dancing in the streets from having won the war. Many also would have disparaged his known communist sympathies.

In fact, Burchett's coverage and its dismissal by the United States might be less significant if other American journalists, including the *New York Times* reporter William H. Lawrence (not to be confused with the paper's science correspondent William "Atomic Bill" Laurence who also figures prominently in this story) had not *also* published articles about the "mysterious" deaths in Hiroshima that same day, which they later recanted.[27] As Burchett was squatting in the rubble of what had been Hiroshima to record his surroundings for his own writing, he looked up to see a small squad of American journalists who had been dispatched from Tokyo by General MacArthur that morning (the day *after* the surrender ceremony), and who arrived on a U.S. Army plane that also brought a small van to shuttle them around the city.

Burchett's recollections of the moment, coupled with Lawrence's article in the *New York Times*, paint a disconcerting picture of American censorship, as he clearly helped the others only to be wholly discredited later—despite having done so because the story he encouraged them to pursue was later determined to be off-limits.[28] Burchett writes that he and his fellow reporters "chatted normally until their officer escorts appeared."[29] Seeing their keepers, the Americans moved away from the Australian and "strolled off taking pictures of the grotesquely twisted girders of the few buildings that had not been melted or pulverized." Even allowing for self-importance, Burchett writes that he had to urge them to go to the hospitals to see "the real story," which at least some did because, in his *New York Times* article, Lawrence explains that doctors in Hiroshima were concerned that everyone who survived the bomb "would die as a result of [its] lingering effects."[30] Devoting even greater attention to medical detail than Burchett did, Lawrence observed that people in Hiroshima "only slightly injured on the day of the blast lost 86 percent of their white blood corpuscles, developed temperatures of 104 degrees Fahrenheit...vomited blood and finally died."

Yet, despite this, Lawrence himself directly disavowed his own words a week later.[31] After a few days back in Tokyo, he sent home a story that ran on the front page of the September 13 paper under the banner headline: "NO RADIOACTIVITY IN HIROSHIMA RUIN." The journalist Amy Goodman observes that this article is bewildering on numerous levels but mainly because "the reporter never mentions his eyewitness account of people dying from radiation sickness which he wrote the previous week."[32] Instead, Lawrence capitulated to governmental pressure or personal conviction or both and repeated verbatim as fact Brigadier General Thomas Farrell's denial given at a press conference that the Army had convened in Tokyo specifically to renounce Burchett's article in the London papers. In print, therefore, America's "paper of record" (as historians referred to the *New York Times* for generations) repudiated "'categorically' that the atomic bomb had produced a dangerous, lingering radioactivity in the ruins of the city."[33]

By then, however, this first William Lawrence was already irrelevant to the Hiroshima story, because the famous William "Atomic Bill" Laurence had taken charge, and he would not let go of the shape of the story until his writing about the splendors of nuclear weapons won him the 1946 Pulitzer Prize for reporting. Throughout the 1930s, Laurence worked as the science correspondent for the *New York Times* and was a known supporter of atomic research. In March 1945, General Leslie Groves rewarded his efforts with the opportunity to write press releases on the progress of the atom bomb's top-secret Manhattan Project in the New Mexico desert. That Laurence was on two seemingly incompatible payrolls (the

War Department and a newspaper determined to publish "All the News That's Fit to Print") did not cause ethical problems either for him or the paper, however, where several of his superiors, including the paper's publisher and editor-in-chief, knew of his work for the government.

Most alarming from any standpoint—ethical or practical—and most significant to what Americans would initially understand as nuclear warfare, however, came in Laurence's front-page splash on September 12: "U.S. Atom Bomb Site Belies Tokyo Tales: Tests on New Mexico Range Confirm That Blast, and Not Radiation, Took Toll." The day before the other Lawrence published his self-negating story from Tokyo, "Atomic Bill" proclaimed to his substantial and intelligent readership that any claims about "mysterious deaths" or illnesses were "Japanese propaganda," pure and simple.[34] Of course, at the time, such pejoratives still held formidable powers of persuasion.

Without doubt, Laurence's fabrications helped to propel the basic story line for Hiroshima and Nagasaki that Americans would come to cling to as history at the cost of learning what was actually going on: "the bombs saved lives." Later official American reports would show that during the month following the bombings, radiation sickness killed at least 30 percent of the total dead. Yet, at this moment, the U.S. government and its officially placed mouthpiece at the *New York Times* established as a fact that no one in Hiroshima had died from radiation and that only foreign lies (British or Japanese) suggested otherwise. Into this mix, Americans widely came to believe that the bombs alone ended the war and preempted the likely November land invasion of Japan, with its officially determined estimate of forty-six thousand American casualties.[35] In short, they learned little if anything about the Soviet entry into the war against Japan or about the Japanese government's attempts to surrender, and they learned close to nothing at all about the bombs' ongoing effects because no major paper in the United States printed anything about them.

Throughout these months, Laurence instead churned out the image-laden pieces about the brilliance of atomic weapons that won him fame. Among other things, he used his experience in the plane over Nagasaki—not on the ground below where he had never been—to justify his position in defining bomb history:

> Being close to it and watching it as it was being fashioned into a living thing so exquisitely shaped that any sculptor would be proud to have created it, one felt oneself in the presence of the supernatural. . . . Awe-struck, we watched it shoot upward like a meteor coming from the earth instead of from outer space, becoming ever more alive as it climbed skyward through the white clouds. It was no longer smoke, or dust, or even a cloud of fire. It was a living thing, a new species of being, born right before our incredulous eyes.

For many Americans, Laurence's view from the clouds became the truth of the event and established guidelines at the time for those who have wanted to deny history to the summer of 1945 ever since.

FIGURE 4.7 The sky above Nagasaki, August 1945
(United States Army Archives)

A significant point, however, is that as early as the fall of 1945 and into 1946, while Laurence and others such as President Harry Truman spun tales of the divine creation and purpose of nuclear weapons, several voices in the United States noticed that the Japanese victims were absent in the American narrative. Most famous in this regard would be John Hersey with his long essay, "Hiroshima," in the August 1946 *New Yorker* magazine, which was read in its entirety on ABC radio over four nights, and which Alfred Knopf rushed into book form by October, and the Book-of-the-Month Club then mailed free to members.[36] Hersey's book had such impact because of his attention to Japanese on the ground realized through portraits of regular people. It is interesting to bear in mind, however, that he did not actually make much of radiation sickness per se until the book's last chapter, where it becomes clear that even some who survived the blast were still dying in unusual ways.

As is well known, Harvard University president and wartime atomic policy maker James. B. Conant responded immediately to Hersey's piece by worrying that Americans would read it and lose their nerve for nuclear war by becoming concerned instead with those who died and how they died.[37] In late September 1946 he wrote his friend Harvey Bundy, who had recently served as a close aide to Secretary of War Henry Stimson, to urge action.[38]

Any reader who first encountered Hiroshima through Hersey's work might find the following lines of Conant's letter particularly intriguing:

> This type of sentimentalism . . . is bound to have a great deal of influence on the next generation. The type of person who goes into teaching, particularly school teaching, will be influenced a great deal by this type of argument. . . . A small minority, if it represents the type of person who is both sentimental and verbally minded and in contact with our youth, may result in distortion of history.[39]

Several things jump out at once. First, it is curious that the president of America's most famous institution of learning is so suspicious of critical thinking. Equally noticeable is that, as the president of America's leading research university, he maintained that stories about the bomb's victims would affect only "sentimental and verbally minded" people, since substantial examples to the contrary already existed. Conant's wartime governmental work alone would have made him fully aware that more than 130 scientists involved with the Manhattan Project—people who are not usually described as "verbal" or "sentimental"—had campaigned vigorously against the bomb's use on Japan and Japanese people during the spring and summer of 1945, with the great physicist Leo Szilard leading the charge.[40] Moreover, as would also have been well known to Conant, by late 1945 a group of Manhattan Project members led by Eugene Rabinowitch (and joined by Hans Bethe, Albert Einstein, and others) began publishing the *Bulletin of Atomic Scientists* to educate non-specialists about nuclear weapons and related issues, including radiation. In other words, Conant blanketed those he saw as dangerous to America's future—which, for him, would necessarily be nuclear-armed—in a way that would portray them as the opposite of rational or logical.

Finally, Conant's fear of Hersey's publication and of its readership begs the question of just what kind of "distortion of history" he was talking about. Most assuredly he was not referring to something critics have long noticed about the work itself: that Hersey conjured a disproportionately high number of Christians in Japan to make his characters appealing to Americans, and that his descriptions barely scratched the surface of the horror. Instead, the president of Harvard feared that Hersey's book would move a majority of Americans to decide that they did not want their government or society to move into a nuclear future without learning about what that meant on the ground. In Conant's view, raising such questions was tantamount to treason, which, more than anything else, evokes patterns of wartime Japan.

Needless to say, Conant prevailed, and the view from the clouds took over America's history of Hiroshima. Through Conant's urging, Harvey Bundy chose Henry Stimson to lay the groundwork for what would come to define, by contrast, the reasoned account of America's initial use of nuclear weapons. In February 1947, *Harper's* magazine published Stimson's "The Decision to Use the Atomic Bomb," co-authored without attribution by Bundy's son, twenty-seven—year old McGeorge, who would gain later renown for urging American escalation in Vietnam. Aware that stories from the ground in Hiroshima were causing a stir—what Stimson called "slapdash criticism"—he and Bundy produced a narrative that has endured to this day, no matter how much documentary evidence to the contrary others discover and make public: "No man . . . holding in his hands a weapon . . . [which would] end the war in victory with the least possible cost in the lives of the men in the armies [that he] had helped to raise . . . could have failed to use it." Millions of Americans remain convinced that this explanation equals the history involved, and Conant congratulated Stimson on a job well done: "I believe that if the propaganda against the use of the atomic bomb had been allowed to grow unchecked, the strength of our military position by virtue of having the bomb would have been correspondingly weakened."[41]

Circling back to 1945 for a minute, even the very lowest projection of twenty-thousand American casualties or the standard forty-six thousand is painful to imagine. Yet, as the consensus of American historians who have studied the issue such as Michael Hogan, Martin Sherwin, Kai Bird, Barton Bernstein, J. Samuel Walker, Paul Boyer, Gar Alperovitz, and Robert Messer has demonstrated through copious research on the bombs and the decision to use them, Americans transferred what happened—the destruction of Hiroshima and Nagasaki—for an event that never took place—the proposed land invasion of Japan—to stand in for history. By the early 1950s, the imagined truth was American myth, and in 1959 President Truman wrote for the record that the bombs spared "half a million" American lives, and that he "never lost any sleep over the decision."[42]

Noticeably, over the years, official estimates for Japanese civilian deaths in Hiroshima and Nagasaki have converged at around 370,000 people. Meanwhile, American storytelling has come to count the number of "saved" Americans as high as 1 million. (This number appeared squarely in David McCullough's 1993 Pulitzer

Prize winning biography, *Truman*, despite abundant evidence to the contrary at the time.) Even without getting caught up in the long-standing debate about the military necessity of the bombings, it is astonishing to realize how easily democratically elected politicians and reporters and educators supportive of free speech led reading and thinking Americans away from the issue of radiation to make their political justifications substitute for history.

KUBOYAMA AIKICHI

While the view from the clouds dominated America, an eerie absence of discussion about Hiroshima and Nagasaki pervaded Japan outside the irradiated cities where MacArthur's occupation government controlled publishing houses and newspapers. Compounding matters, the official silence concerning the bomb and its effects became ensconced as legal precedence at the time. In May 1946, on the fifth day of proceedings for the International Military Tribunal for the Far East (known as the Tokyo Trials or Japan's Nuremburg), one of the five American-appointed lawyers for the defense, Ben Bruce Blakeney, questioned the notion that killing in war constituted murder, which, in turn, challenged the legality of the prosecution's charges and of the tribunal itself.[43] In the midst of a courtroom packed with Japanese spectators who anticipated that the American lawyers would do nothing substantial for the Japanese men they were to defend, Blakeney announced in a calm, firm voice: "The very existence of the entire body of international law on the subject of war gives evidence of the legality of war. . . . The proposition that killing in war is not murder *that killing in war is not murder* follows from the fact that war is legal." He followed by thinking aloud to the court that charging an individual with crimes against peace was creating a new category of criminal. If this were to be the case, as it appeared to be, Blakeney continued, "if the bombing of Pearl Harbor is murder, we know the name of the very man whose hands loosed the atomic bomb on Hiroshima. We know the name of the Chief of Staff who planned that act. We know the chief of the responsible stages. Is murder on their consciences? We may well doubt it." His words were never translated into Japanese at the trial, and his comments disappeared from the printed record. Moreover, as we all know, Blakeney's legal gambit failed. Truman was not tried as a war criminal, and nuclear weapons came to generate their own de facto legitimacy, standing today as the international community's legal weapon of mass destruction.

Surprisingly, in 1954, a random accident in the middle of the Pacific Ocean changed the boundaries of official denial about the bomb, and, in simplest terms, made it more difficult for Washington as well as other governments to turn away completely from the realities of nuclear warfare. Unlike the debate that still persists (in the United States at least) about whether the atomic bombs used against Japanese civilians were aimed at military targets, there could be no such discussion about the purpose of the hydrogen bombs developed soon thereafter. The destructive possibilities of these weapons preempted arguments about their potential targets, because they were designed (and still are) to annihilate entire populations. Most famously, even the creator of the original bomb, J. Robert Oppenheimer, who reveled while watching the Trinity Test in July 1945 by quoting from an ancient Hindu text—"Now I am become death, the destroyer of worlds"—learned from the human costs at Hiroshima and Nagasaki and protested Washington's development of the hydrogen bomb.[44] The problem was, however, that although Oppenheimer regretted the use of his science once it was clear to him what it could and would do, the bomb wasn't "his" anymore. By 1954, during the height of McCarthyism, the so-called father of the atomic bomb himself had become a suspicious American for challenging what was fast becoming the American way of life.

If most Americans are unlikely to know the details behind the decision to bomb Hiroshima and Nagasaki, they are much less likely to know about America's subsequent use of nuclear weapons in the Marshall Islands from 1946 to 1958. Despite this awareness gap, the anthropologist Holly Barker, who has spent decades in these islands, argues that "the United States achieved its global superpower status *as a result of* its weapons testing in the Marshall Islands."[45] Since the test explosions themselves register so minutely, if at all, on the radar screens of many Americans of the twentieth century, Barker's statement might sound outrageous to some. Yet, the logic she argues rests on the palpable fear that the *threat* of thermonuclear destruction generated for so much of the world during the second half of the twentieth century, making her assertion not so outlandish after all. Most important for us to think about is how American nuclear weapons testing in the South Pacific threaded itself into the knot already tying the United States together with Japan and Korea, only further complicating it and America's history out of bounds.

Washington's preparations for weapons testing in the Marshall Islands began almost as soon as Japan surrendered in August 1945, with American political and military leaders eager to show off their new power to all who wanted to see. The island setting would allow representatives from around the world to watch the explosions against a blank backdrop—or at least one that would appear to have no history—which was, of course, the opposite of seeing the living and dying reality of Hiroshima and Nagasaki at the time. In other words, all awe and no mess. In July 1946, the U.S. government invited more than one hundred diplomats, generals, and scientists to stand aboard observation ships near Bikini atoll and watch the first test, self-consciously named "Operation Crossroads."

Although officials repeatedly stated that the purpose of the test was only to demonstrate the science and not to threaten anyone, everyone understood, by watching the test, that the Americans were invincible, at least for the moment. And although the American government repeatedly announced that there were no dangers involved in the tests, later that month the second blast of the series churned out all sorts of inconveniently unpredicted by-products, causing the cancellation of the scheduled third test and exposing the forty thousand participating U.S. troops to radioactive fallout, which Robert Stone's 1987 film *Radio Bikini* stunningly demonstrates.[46] After this mishap, Washington was much less eager to display America's tests in real time and routinely created giant no-go zones in the Pacific Ocean around the islands, continually relocating Marshallese islanders from one spot to the next while blowing up their native lands.

Poisonous debris was part and parcel of the sixty-seven different tests that continued until 1958 (equaling in total about seven thousand Hiroshimas), a reality Henry Kissinger infamously defended by saying, "There are only ninety thousand people out there. Who gives a damn?"[47] As a result, the Marshallese have long been suing the U.S. government to apologize and provide compensation for the illnesses and premature deaths caused by the weapons as well as the whole-scale degradation and destruction of their country.

In the midst of the testing program in 1954, during a brief moment that would ultimately give the Marshallese basis for their subsequent claims, one explosion went completely out of control and ended up killing a Japanese fisherman. When the U.S. government stepped in to make amends for the situation, Washington created guidelines—inadvertently or not—for coping with the civilian casualties that U.S. military actions would cause in the new era of nuclear warfare. Noticeably, the American government's only partial extension of justice at the time of the 1954 accident affirmed what would become an official inability to deal comprehensively with related histories, foreign or domestic. Moreover, the Japanese government's compliance with the United States at this juncture set in motion the self-perpetuating cycle of avoidance at the official level that continues to this day.

As is well known, in March 1954 the fifteen-megaton *Bravo* explosion generated far greater force than anyone predicted. One thousand times the power of the Hiroshima bomb, *Bravo* spewed fallout over a much larger area than the military's established perimeter. The white coral reefs in the area dissolved into an irradiated, fine white powder that came to be known as the "ashes of death." The ash rained down on the crews of at least twenty Japanese fishing boats within a hundred miles of the test, showered at least three hundred Marshallese who had already been relocated from their homes to so-called safe places, and coated about thirty American Marines involved in conducting the experiment.

Within several months, one of the Japanese fishermen, Kuboyama Aikichi, died from radiation illness. His plight set in motion two opposing concerns that rotated around the same issue. On one end of the spectrum, the circumstances of Kuboyama's illness and death created the first widespread, public effort anywhere in Asia to hold the U.S. government accountable for civilian deaths and injuries caused by American military actions. On the other end, Washington's response to Kuboyama's death entrenched legal maneuverability for those who would justify America's use of nuclear weapons across time.

It is important to bear in mind that there was no large-scale Japanese movement (or any other) to ban nuclear weapons after

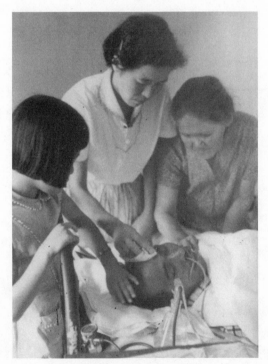

FIGURE 4.8 Kuboyama Aikichi at death, 1954
(Daigo Fukuryu Maru Exhibition Hall Collection, Tokyo)

their initial use on the civilian populations of Hiroshima and Nagasaki in 1945, let alone to seek American atonement for having done so. This does not mean that Japanese meekly accepted the fact of being the world's first victims of nuclear warfare. At the end of the war, however, the combination for most Japanese of needing to survive—which included competing for already scarce resources with the waves of repatriates from Japan's collapsed Asian empire (roughly one-tenth of the population of 70 million at the time)—and of believing the most horrible rumors about the survivors of Hiroshima and Nagasaki was enough to make many Japanese complacent with the U.S. occupation's informational black hole about the bomb.

By 1954, however, when the Japanese fisherman sailing aboard a trawler called the *Lucky Dragon* became the world's first known victim of a hydrogen bomb, conditions in Japan were very different and allowed many Japanese to openly question America's nuclear program writ large. To begin with, survival for many Japanese now

FIGURE 4.9 Contaminated tuna, 1954
(Daigo Fukuryu Maru Exhibition Hall Collection, Tokyo)

FIGURE 4.10 Signatures being collected
in Tokyo of those opposed to nuclear bombs, 1954
(Daigo Fukuryu Maru Exhibition Hall Collection, Tokyo)

meant getting up early enough to catch the right train to get to work
on time. Also important, when the American occupation ended in
1952, so did its censorship of the atomic bombings, meaning that by
1954, when Kuboyama Aikichi became ill and died before the nation's eyes, many Japanese had read about and seen photographs of
the 1945 blasts in Hiroshima and Nagasaki and were also aware that
many Japanese were still plagued by similar illnesses from that earlier history. On top of this, and pushing matters over the edge for
most, nine tons of contaminated tuna from this fisherman's boat
alone (others were hit, too) were sold and consumed by hundreds
across the country.[48]

Two months after the *Bravo* test, in May 1954 a group of house-wives in Tokyo's Suginami district began collecting signatures to demand that the Japanese government do something to protest the actions of the United States.[49] The Suginami Appeal, as it became known, sparked a national campaign that amassed almost 15 million signatures by August 1954 and spawned the first World Conference against Atomic and Hydrogen Bombs in August 1955 (by which time the Appeal had collected signatures from over half of Japan's registered voters).[50]

Like South Korea's 2002–2003 protests against American military violence, Japan's 1954 Suginami Appeal became a matter of middle-class concern, meaning that even Japan's very pro-American prime minister, Yoshida Shigeru, had to respond. Fortunately for Yoshida, the U.S. government was more than eager to defuse the situation for him, and on January 4, 1955, the American ambassador to Japan, John Allison, wrote Japanese Foreign Minister Shigemitsu Mamoru to explain the terms of America's atonement:

> Your Excellency knows of the deep concern and sincere regret the Government and people of the United States of America have manifested over the injuries suffered by Japanese fishermen in the course of these tests, and of the earnest hopes held in the United States for the welfare and well-being of these injured fishermen. The Government of the United States of America has made clear that it is prepared to make monetary compensation as an additional expression of its concern and regret over the injuries sustained.[51]

The United States would disburse $2 million to the Japanese government to pay roughly $20,000 to each fisherman aboard the *Lucky Dragon*. Fifty years later, a former schoolteacher and local activist from the fishing boat's home port of Yaizu in Shizuoka prefecture described how this money made unaffected fishermen jealous of the sick ones because they all had fallen into poverty as a result of the national fish boycott after the *Bravo* test. As he recalled, some of the local women exclaimed, "I wish my husband had been showered with radioactive ash."[52]

The whole event spread more than just awareness about financial payments and apology as a means of redress: it marked the first time that a broadly popular movement resulted in the United States accepting responsibility for foreign civilian casualties of U.S. military action. But this was not simply a routine victory for activists, for Washington at once wrapped Tokyo into the terms of its settlement. Shigemitsu's acceptance of Allison's note and its provisions meant "the full settlement of any and all claims against the United States" and "confirmation of these mutual understandings of our Governments." In turn this came to mean, in practical terms, that other deaths from related nuclear histories such as Hiroshima or Nagasaki would remain out of bounds, a condition the government of Japan has upheld to this day.

LEGAL MASS DESTRUCTION

In mid-February 2002, President George Bush visited Tokyo during the first of his two state trips to Asia. He and his advisers hoped to accomplish all sorts of things, from launching plans for the 150-year anniversary of Japanese-American relations to thanking the Japanese government for its financial and logistical support of America's War on Terror. Officials also wanted to calm anxieties that had sprung up throughout the region following the American president's surprise inclusion of North Korea in his now infamous "axis of evil" speech a month earlier.

Bush arrived in Tokyo on a warm, clear day, one that I remember well because, thanks to his visit, I had an unexpected, theatrical education in one of the trajectories of Hiroshima's history during my routine walk to the archives. As I headed down the main boulevard near Japan's parliament building and across the street from the National Library, several of the notorious black trucks popular with the country's extreme right wing passed me by with the lead van blaring the customary martial songs. This was not unusual, but the message pouring from the loud speakers of the second truck stopped me flat: "Welcome to Japan, President Bush of the United States of America! Apologize for Hiroshima and enjoy your stay!" I stood there stunned for a moment; it seemed as if the sum total of avoiding history everywhere was landing at my feet.

Throughout the recent era of apologies all around—or maybe in spite of it—there has remained one matter on which Washington holds firm, regardless of who is in office: there will be no apology for Hiroshima or Nagasaki. Most noticeable was Bill Clinton's powerful delivery of the national line in April 1995: "The United States owes no apology to Japan for having dropped the atomic bombs on Hiroshima and Nagasaki."[53] Perhaps these words reverberated so strongly because Clinton had been surprisingly vocal in offering other apologies during his presidency: for the Tuskegee Syphilis Study, for example, for "European Americans receiving the fruits of the slave trade," or for U.S. sponsorship of right-wing governments in Guatemala, all of which usefully challenged other American narratives.[54]

Clinton's statement about the history of Hiroshima and Nagasaki did not distinguish him from his predecessors. Yet, as the first president born after 1945, his words reveal America's dependency on the "saved lives" rhetoric more than anything else. Put differently, unlike the others, Clinton would not be able to recall for the nation where he was that August morning, or how grateful he felt that the war was over, or any of the other usual ways of explaining away Hiroshima's history on the ground. As a result, the question of why this history remains so untouchable *again* comes back to us. If, as Clinton demonstrated, he was willing to tackle other contentious histories such as slavery and its ongoing legacies, or the issue of America's blind support of anything "anticommunist" during the Cold War era, what keeps the nation's nuclear history so off-limits?

The chronic inability to confront how America's use of nuclear weapons against Japanese people in 1945 might constitute the kind of history for which survivors would seek an apology, let alone why the use of such weapons might represent a crime against humanity, is sustained by Washington's determination to maintain these weapons as the once and future legitimate tools of the national arsenal. It is not at all by chance that among weapons of mass destruction—nuclear, chemical, and biological—only nuclear weapons are *not* prohibited in international law.[55] Were it otherwise, the likelihood that the history of America's use of them on Japan would generate charges of attempted genocide against the United States or Harry Truman would increase exponentially.

This remains improbable, however, not in the least because the Japanese government continues to abet this dynamic. The mayors of Hiroshima and Nagasaki have famously traveled to the International Court of Justice at The Hague where they have made impassioned pleas about the illegality of nuclear weapons on behalf of their constituencies' history and on the future of humanity. In response, representatives from Tokyo's Foreign Ministry stand up and explain that although such statements are were quite moving they do not represent the official Japanese view. Then everyone sits down. As matters remain, only the government of Japan could charge the United States with the illegal use of nuclear weapons against civilians in war. Meanwhile, its leaders feed Washington's view from the clouds by not doing so.

As Japan's desired world posture has increased with its economic prowess, America's rigidity about the nation's historical use of atomic weapons against Japan has increasingly played into the hands of hard-liners who urge Japan to stand on its own, regardless of U.S. policy, along the lines of "Japan That Can Say No." Essential to this trend has been the co-option of Japan's atomic history away from traditionally left-leaning groups for very different purposes. Official Japan used to regard the sometimes openly anti-American and openly pro-communist (or at least pro-socialist) "NO MORE HIROSHIMAS!" demonstrations of the 1960s and 1970s as a threat to Japanese society. Today, however, such sentiment is not considered violent coming from the other direction. Different from the riot police that once surrounded Japan's long-gone leftist protestors, not even one patrol car followed the black sound trucks and their menacing anti-American message on that February day in 2002, which was only noticeable because President Bush was so physically nearby.

Maybe everyone was hoping no one would hear, or, if they did, that they would not understand Japanese.

And Now

More than sixty years of political apologies and apologetic narratives have woven Japan, Korea, and the United States together into a sea of stories in which blame and denial masquerade as history. National storytellers name one side guilty and another innocent, which intensifies the "us versus them" divide on which national "isms" and identities are bred and encourages mythmakers to spin larger and larger tales to preach as their peoples' truth. But that's the name of the game, and there's a lot of money to be made by keeping it going.

Global capital, of course, produces ever more volatile combinations to feed the "history problems." Increased possibilities for learning in terms of travel and translations, for example, mix with a growing unease for most about jobs, futures, and a place to call "home." The nation's gatekeepers have had to redouble efforts to shore up their narratives lest they lose control entirely, all of which would help explain the recent trend of apologies all around because saying sorry for certain histories gained traction once those making the apologies discovered in them a means with which to reinstate the nation in the international system.

Practicing apologies in such a way did not necessitate that they ring hollow, yet recent apologies have largely fallen short of what those seeking them wanted, which, ironically, often amounted to being dignified *within* the narrative that was eliding or maligning their mention in the first place. A main reason why so many of the apologies failed to calm problematic pasts is that their scriptwriters found themselves so deeply ensconced or trapped within prevailing national myths that they could not tell enough of the truth to make the particular apology hold, which is especially noticeable in demands from one nation to another.

Along these lines, when the U.S. House of Representatives passed H. Res. 121 on July 30, 2007, calling on the government of Japan to apologize for the comfort women system, it should have come as no surprise that the government of Japan would balk, responding in different ways depending on individual leanings. Hard-liners railed against the resolution's sponsor, California Democrat Mike Honda, in entirely racist terms as a disgruntled ethnic minority who was anti- "real" Japanese or as a pawn of Chinese and Korean interests. They missed the point, of course, because to the contrary Mike Honda is as decent a politician as any democracy could hope for, and perhaps most closely resembles the Japanese historian Ienaga Saburo with his high school history teacher's unwavering determination to bring truth to light. Obviously, the reaction of the Far Right seemed logical only to those already convinced that Japan had done nothing wrong.

Japan's centrist and mildly left-leaning opposition led by Ozawa Ichiro, however, got straight to the point and insistently called on Japan's ruling party and the then prime minister Abe to demand an apology from the United States for the atomic bombings of Hiroshima and Nagasaki. Amid all this, and owing to various other factors (mainly money scandals), Ozawa's party won a landslide parliamentary victory, and there is talk now of a counter resolution from the party calling for an American apology. Should this occur, it could pass because even those on the other end of Japan's political spectrum have discovered a way to use the atomic histories for themselves.

In the end, the survivors of last century's atrocities, such as the former comfort women and the bomb victims, most powerfully destabilize the myths that continue to ignore or belittle their claims to make sense of themselves. Against the grain of the fables that would deny them, however, it remains possible to address their histories honestly. Doing so now would allow those who suffered to have a say in shaping how the story gets told, whereas avoiding matters merely puts things on hold for a future where any meaningful apology would only dissipate in the air.

This book is about the ownership of memory & history; consequences of ingenuine apology

NOTES

1. AN ISLAND BY ANY OTHER NAME

1. On June 9, 1948, an American bomber discharged its cargo over the islands. Some maintain that the plane purposefully targeted fishermen on the rocks and in boats, but others claim it was accidental. Casualty estimates range from around thirty to more than three hundred dead, and during August 2006 a South Korean research team fished bomb shards and unexploded ordinance out of the nearby waters (Korean Broadcasting System, August 2, 2006).

2. See coverage throughout February and March 2005 in the *Asahi Shimbun* and the *Hankyoreh*, as well as in the English-language dailies the *Japan Times* and the *Korea Herald*.

3. *Korea Herald*, February 23, 2005.

4. On the president's official homepage, "Dokdo: Historic Land" archives statements about Korea's claims, http://english.president.go.kr/ (accessed April 10, 2006).

5. The most articulate example of this viewpoint is Victor D. Cha, *Alignment Despite Antagonism: The United States–Korea–Japan Security Triangle* (Stanford: Stanford University Press, 1999).

6. Walter Benjamin, "Theses on the Philosophy of History," quoted in Moishe Postone, "The Holocaust and the Trajectory of the Twentieth Century," in Moishe Postone and Eric Santner, eds., *Catastrophe and Meaning: The Holocaust and the Twentieth Century* (Chicago: University of Chicago Press, 2003), p. 103.

7. Harry Harootunian, "Japan's Long Postwar: The Trick of Memory and the Ruse of History," *South Atlantic Quarterly* 99, no. 4 (Fall 2000): 715–739, esp. 719–720.

8. See William Underwood, "Names, Bones, and Unpaid Wages: Reparations for Korean Forced Labor in Japan," parts 1 and 2, posted to Japan Focus, September 2006, http://www.japanfocus.org/products/details/2219; see also Oguri Kohei's brilliant 1984 film, *Kayako no tame ni* (For Kayako).

9. See the English Web site for the Seoul Metropolitan Government Parks and Landscape Office, "Soedaemun Prison History Hall," http://parks.seoul.go.kr/main/english/independence/prison.htm (accessed January 20, 2006).

10. See http://www.kaijipr.or.jp (accessed February 10, 2006).

11. Amino wrote more than twenty books and one hundred articles, yet almost none has been translated and published in its entirety in English. In Japanese, among his most important essays is "Nihon Rettō to Sono Shūhen: 'Nihon ron' no Genzai" (The Japanese Archipelago and Its Surrounding Area), in *Iwanami Kōza Nihon Tsushi*, vol. 1, *Nihon Rettō to Jinrui Shakai* (The Japanese Archipelago and Its People and Society) (Tokyo: Iwanami Shoten, 1993), pp. 5–37. See William Johnston's thoughtful consideration of Amino's life and work, "From Feudal Fishing Villages to an Archipelago's People: The Historiographical Journey of Amino Yoshihiko," Harvard University, Reischauer Institute Occasional Papers in Japanese Studies, March 2005.

12. See http://www.umimori.jp (accessed January 20, 2006).

13. Funabashi Yoichi, http://www.asahi.com/column/funabashi/eng (accessed March 5, 2006).

14. Tessa Morris-Suzuki, *The Past Within Us: Media, Memory, History* (New York: Verso, 2005), p. 218.

15. Google it. Naver it. Yafuu it. That's the point.

16. See http://www.mofa.go.jp/region/asia-paci/takeshima/position.html; http://www.mofat.go.kr/index.jsp (both accessed January 15, 2006).

17. The Japanese government's Web site has been updated since and made more elaborate with new maps and charts. More polished and better designed, it nonetheless retains if not amplifies the same logic.

18. The Korean site has also been updated, yet it archives its position papers and official statements online. Search for July 18, 2005, position report.

19. To reiterate, the Japanese site has been updated, yet throughout these pages I quote from the 2005 version as it appeared then. The text of the new Japanese version (as well as its English translation page) includes minor differences in wording—in this case, in English, "an integral part"

has become "an inherent part"—and in some cases the argument has been substantially lengthened. The line of reasoning, however, follows the contours of its earlier version. For its part, the Korean site archives its July 2005 paper.

20. Given that the Japanese government has *clearly* paid attention to this Web site since 2005 and has *clearly* spent a good amount of tax-payer money in revising it, its continued failure to mention Japan's colonization of Korea between 1905 and 1945 is especially noticeable.

21. See http://www.isop.ucla.edu/eas/documents/peace1951.htm (accessed February 1, 2006).

22. Japan's updated Web site refers to American occupation rule of the area as "an interim cessation by Japan of the exercise of governmental or administrative authority."

23. The updated Web site has dropped this sentence. The more recent version, accessed August 5, 2007, continues to blur the issue by justifying its position on two pieces of correspondence dating from July 1951 between Seoul and Washington. As with its earlier paper, however, the Japanese government has overlooked the inner workings of the moment, using the end product to define the historical process.

24. Although the revised Japanese Web site now quotes this SCAP order, it denies history to the moment by concluding that, since the San Francisco Treaty superseded the orders, "none of the treatment of Takeshima prior to the effect of that Treaty affects the attribution issue of Takeshima."

25. United States, State Department Record Group 59, General Records of the Department of State, Records of the U.S. Department of State Relating to the Internal Affairs of Japan, 1945–1954, Washington, D.C., Diplomatic Branch, National Archives. Cited also in Cheong Sung-hwa, *The Politics of Anti-Japanese Sentiment in Korea: Japanese-South Korean Relations under the American Occupation, 1945–1952* (Westport, Conn.: Greenwood, 1991), chap. 3.

26. Washington's side of the 1951 correspondence that the government of Japan uses on its updated Web site quotes from this document.

27. William Sebald's commentary on the sixth draft of the treaty quoted in Kajimura Hideki, "The Question of Takeshima/Tokdo," in *Chōsen Kenkyū*, no. 182 (September 1978); reprinted in *Korea Observer* 28, no. 3 (Autumn 1997): 462, and in Kim Young Koo, *A Pursuit of Truth in the Dokdo Island Issue: Letters to a Young Japanese Man* (Seoul: Bub Young Sa, 2003), p. 5 n. 5. Professor Kim also has his own Web site devoted to the island debate, http://www.kocean

.org. Recently, the South Korean newspaper *Segye Ilbo* reported on a 1954 report in which General James A. Van Fleet urged President Eisenhower to continue U.S. support of Japanese control of the disputed islands. The monumental "Report of the Van Fleet Mission to the Far East" is catalogued in the George C. Marshall Library and was declassified in 1986. As far as the islands are concerned, Van Fleet follows the contours of Sebald's note and the San Francisco Treaty.

28. *Korea Herald*, March 2005.

29. Although the islands were in the American-occupied Korean zone, the occupation authorities issued no-go instructions only in Japanese to Japanese fishermen.

30. The Japanese government's revised Web site (accessed August 5, 2007) newly addresses this thorn in a specially boxed explanation at the bottom of its page called "Self-Restraint on the Issue of Entering Takeshima from the ROK Mainland." For some at least, however, its words would suggest more than diplomatic niceties: "Under the circumstances in which the illegal occupation of Takeshima by the ROK persisits [*sic*], the entry of Japanese nationals to Takeshima via the ROK mainland might give wrong impressions that the Japanese nationals admit that they are subject to the jurisdiction of the ROK in Takeshima and that they recognize the ROK's sovereignty over Takeshima. The understanding and cooperation of the people of Japan on this point are therefore requested."

31. See http://www.mofa.go.jp/policy/maritime/japan/index.html; http://www.mofat.go.kr/pdffiles/Eastsea1.pdf (both accessed March 15, 2006).

32. Unlike the Takeshima site, the government of Japan has not substantially changed the Sea of Japan page.

33. See http://www.dokdomuseum.go.kr/ (accessed March 10, 2006).

34. There are some wonderful Dokdo songs, including "Dokdo Is Our Land" (*Dokdo nun uri ttang imnida*) linked to the Cyber Dokdo Web site under "*Dokdo noreh*." If you do not read Korean, look for the button decorated with stereo equipment on the right-hand side, in the middle of the page, http://www.dokdo.go.kr (accessed March 10, 2006).

35. It is important to note that a political party that descended from former president Kim Dae-jung, the architect of current unification policy, was called the Uri Party.

36. *Asahi Shimbun*, January 8, 2007.

37. *Asahi Shimbun*, August 20, 2002.

1. The note is catalogued among papers at Yale University's Manuscripts and Archives collection: Horace Capron Papers, no. 128, Box 1, Folders 14, 15.

2. Norma Field, "War and Apology: Japan, Asia, the Fiftieth, and After," in "The Comfort Women: Colonialism, War, and Sex," ed. Choi Chungmoo, special issue, *Positions: East Asia Cultures Critique* 5, no. 1 (Spring 1997): 5.

3. For a well-written example, see Funabashi Yoichi, "Kako Kokufuku Seisaku o Teisho Suru,"(A Proposal for a Policy to Overcome the Past), *Sekai*, no. 692 (2001): 48–62, esp. 50–51.

4. *Asahi Shimbun*, February 21, 1965.

5. September 6, 1984, Reception at the Imperial Palace, Tokyo. For a useful compendium, see Arai Shinichi and Iko Toshiya, "Compendium List of Apologies," *Sekai* (World), no. 696 (December 2001): 178–196.

6. Michael Frayn's elaboration of Willy Brandt's gesture in his 2004 play, *Democracy*, raises still important questions of its motivation, timing, and reception.

7. In an essay discussing Korean soldiers in the Japanese Army, the wonderful social critic Utsumi Aiko observes that, "in exchange for not having to learn military patriotism, I also never learned about the history of Japan's war of invasion." See Utsumi Aiko, "Korean 'Imperial Soldiers': Remembering Colonialism and Crimes against Allied POWs," in T. Fujitani, Geoffrey M. White, Lisa Yoneyama, eds., *Perilous Memories: The Asia-Pacific War(s)* (Durham: Duke University Press, 2001), p. 200.

8. W. G. Sebald, *On the Natural History of Destruction* (New York: Penguin, 2004), p. 4. Robert Moeller has drawn important attention to some of the troubling consequences of the recent trend toward re-remembering the bombings of German cities. See Moeller, "On the History of Man-made Destruction: Loss, Death, Memory, and Germany in the Bombing War," *History Workshop Journal*, no. 61 (Fall 2006): 103–134.

9. Sebald, *On the Natural History of Destruction*, p. 4.

10. Ibid., pp. 13–14.

11. Ibid., pp. 11–12.

12. John Treat, *Writing Ground Zero: Japanese Literature and the Atomic Bomb* (Chicago: University of Chicago Press, 1996).

13. Article III of Ito Hirobumi, *Commentaries on the Constitution of the Empire of Japan* (1889), translated by Ito Miyoji (Tokyo: Chuo University Press, 1906), p. 2.

14. *New York Times*, January 1, 1946. This sentence is taken from a larger proclamation that historians call "Emperor Hirohito's Rescript Disavowing His Own Divinity." Japan's Minister of Education at the time, Maeda Tamon, wrote the document and discussed working with Hirohito on it in a 1962 article in the Japanese magazine *Bungei Shunjū*. See Maeda Tamon, "*Ningen sengen no uchi-soto*," (The Inside Story of the Emperor's Declaration), *Bungei Shunjū*, March 1962.

15. General Douglas MacArthur to Chief of Staff Eisenhower, Telegram, January 25, 1946, collected in U.S. Department of State, *Foreign Relations of the United States, 1945*, Vol. 8, *The Far East* (Washington, D.C.: State Department/GPO, 1971), p. 395.

16. The most comprehensive discussion in English is Herbert Bix, *Hirohito and the Making of Modern Japan* (New York: Harper's, 2001).

17. See "What Do You Tell the Dead When You Lose?" in John Dower, *Embracing Defeat: Japan in the Wake of World War II* (New York: Norton, 1999), chap. 9.

18. Former Japanese soldiers who have come forward during recent years to testify about the comfort woman system make this abundantly clear. See, for example, Matsui Minoru, *Riben Guizi* (*Japanese Devils*) (Tokyo: Directors System, 2001); Nancy Tong, *In the Name of the Emperor* (New York: Film News Now Foundation, 1996).

19. Jeffrey Olick, "Genre Memories and Memory Genres: A Dialogical Analysis of May 8, 1945 Commemorations in the Federal Republic of Germany," *American Sociological Review* 64 (1999): 381–402, quote at 382.

20. *Asahi Shimbun*, December 6, 2004.

21. *Asahi Shimbun*, March 9, 2006.

22. *Asahi Shimbun*, December 17, 2006.

23. Arai and Iko, "Compendium List of Apologies," p. 194.

24. Only the rarest of Japanese politicians has publicly noticed that the rhetoric of "sorrow and regret" itself sustains the problems. On the eve of the inauguration of South Korean president Roh Moo-hyun, Japanese parliamentarian Okazaki Tomoko visited Seoul to speak with him. Later, she informed reporters that she "requested (President-elect) Roh to take the [comfort women] issue seriously. As Roh emphasizes a 'future-oriented' relationship, I pointed out that the future can only begin after clearing up the past." Quoted in the *Korea Herald*, February 13, 2003.

25. The tragic June 1948 bombing by the U.S. Air Force of the Korean fishermen on the islands contested between Japan and South Korea

happened because neither the U.S. military authority in Korea nor the Koreans themselves understood the details of MacArthur's fishing guidelines for Japan.

26. On July 27, 1953, delegates met at Panmunjom to formalize the armistice. Nam Il, a North Korean general, and William K. Harrison Jr., Lieutenant General of the U.S. Army, signed the paper. Although Harrison signed on behalf of the United Nations, the Americans took charge of the South's decision.

27. United Nations, *Treaty Series: Treaties and International Agreements Registered or Filed and Recorded with the Secretariat of the United Nations*, Vol. 583 (New York: United Nations Publications, 1966).

28. In May 1964, for example, the National Security Council staff member Robert Komer wrote to the National Security Adviser McGeorge Bundy: "We're still spending over $300 million a year on 20 million ROKs with really no end in sight. So we've got to find someone to share the long-term burden, and it's logically the Japs." Catalogued in Karen L. Gatz, ed., *Foreign Relations of the United States, 1964–1968*, Vol. 29, pt. 1, Korea (Washington, D.C.: U.S. Government Printing Office, 2000), p. 760.

29. For a compelling discussion of Japan's formula for redress in Southeast Asia, see Sayuri Shimizu, *Creating a People of Plenty: The United States and Japan's Economic Alternatives, 1950–1960* (Kent, Ohio: Kent State University Press, 2001), esp. chap. 4.

30. In Gatz, *Foreign Relations of the United States*, No. 349, Reischauer to Rusk, September 8, 1964, p. 770.

31. Ibid., No. 353, Reischauer to Rusk, November 21, 1964, p. 778.

32. *Asahi Shimbun*, February 17, 1965, front page, evening edition.

33. Ibid.

34. In Gatz, *Foreign Relations of the United States*, No. 357, Thomson to McGeorge Bundy, February 20, 1965, p. 784.

35. Okuda Masanori, "Sengo Hosho Saiban no Doko to Rippoteki Kaiketsu," (Movements in Postwar Compensation Decisions and Their Legal Interpretations), in Chi Myon Gwan, Igarashi Masahiro, et al., *Nikkan no Sogo Rikai to Sengo Hosho (New Japan-Korea Partnership and Postwar Compensation)* (Tokyo: Nihon Hyoronsha, 2002), pp. 131–146, and especially the useful chronological chart of claims against Japan from 1990 to the present, pp. 147–159.

36. See coverage in *Asahi Shimbun*, October 9, 1998; *Chosun Ilbo*, October 9,1998; and the *New York Times*, October 9, 1998. The full text is in Arai

and Iko, "Compendium List of Aplogies," p. 195; for the English translation, see http://www.mofa.go.jp/region/asiapaci/korea/joint9810.html (accessed January 10, 2007).

37. During preparation for the most recent normalization talks in August 2002, North Korea's demands for apology and reparations emerged as a chief obstacle. See *Asahi Shimbun*, August 26, 2002.

38. Michael Robinson has written extensively on Japan's self-consciously launched era of "cultural sharing" during its colonial rule of Korea. See Robinson, "Broadcasting, Cultural Hegemony, and Colonial Modernity in Korea, 1924–1945," in Gi-Wook Shin and Michael Robinson, eds., *Colonial Modernity in Korea* (Cambridge, Mass.: Harvard University Press, 1999), pp. 52–69.

39. See Koichi Iwabuchi's fascinating analysis of this moment as a "Return to Asia" in "Nostalgia for a (Different) Asian Modernity: Media Consumption of 'Asia' in Japan," *Positions: East Asia Cultures Critique* 10, no. 3 (Winter 2002): 547–573.

40. Google him. There are more than a million sites in English alone.

41. Rakuen Korea, Inc., was the first to realize the trend as it was one of the only registered companies that introduced Japanese women and South Korean men when the "Yon-sama" craze first broke. The company reported eighty requests in October 2003 and seventeen hundred in April 2004, with the spike coming right after the mega-star visited Japan. See Sakagami Yasuko's online reports on the Nipponia Web site among others.

42. According to the Korean National Tourist Organization, the number of Japanese tourists to Chunchon jumped from 40,000 to 140,000 in a single year.

43. Diane Lee, "Winter Sonata Drama Fever," posted to UniOrb, January 31, 2005, http://uniorb.com/ATREND/Japanwatch/wsdramafever.htm.

44. Yamano Sharin, *Manga Kenkanryū* (*Hating the Korean Wave*) (Tokyo: Shinyusha, 2005).

45. *Asahi Shimbun*, September 17, 2002.

46. See David McNeill, "Selective Pain: Kidnapping, Contemporary Japan, and Media Obsession," posted to Japan Focus, August 6, 2006, http://www.japanfocus.org/products/details/2231.

47. Charles Jenkins published his story in Japanese in 2005 and in Korean the following year. There is still no English translation of his story, titled *To Tell the Truth*. See Jenkins, *Kokuhaku* (Tokyo: Kadokawa Shoten, 2005). A Web site called Black Ship features a number of photos from the

book as well as sections in English translation, http://www.imbermedia
.net/politics/en/ (accessed January 20, 2007).

48. See philosopher Takahashi Tetsuya's powerful comment in "Koreans under Assault from the Japanese Right," *Hankyoreh*, March 12, 2007.

49. A year after the senior foreign ministry official Tanaka Hitoshi paved the way for Koizumi's historic visit to Pyongyang, members of a group known as "The Brigade for Conquering North Korea" hurled firebombs at his house to protest his "treacherous" acts. Tanaka has since been forced out of public service. See Tessa Morris-Suzuki's succinct summary of the September 2003 attack, "When Is a Terrorist Not a Terrorist?" posted to Japan Focus, October 10, 2003, http://www.japanfocus
.org/products/details/1838.

50. Kobayashi Yoshinori, *Sensōron* (On War) (Tokyo: Gentosha, 1998); Kobayashi Yoshinori, *Sensōron* 2 (On War 2) (Tokyo: Gentosha, 2001). For a thoughtful discussion, see Rebecca Clifford, "Cleansing History, Cleansing Japan: Kobayashi Yoshinori's Analects of War and Japan's Revisionist Revival," in Oxford University's Nissan Occasional Papers Series, 2004.

51. Kobayashi, *Sensōron*, p. 19.

52. Ibid., pp. 196–197; Kobayashi, *Sensōron* 2, p. 91.

53. One group led by Umeno Masanobu and Sawada Tatsuo protested their opposition to Kobayashi in a volume entitled *Sensōron/Mosoron* (Tokyo: Kyoiku Shiryo Shuppankai, 1999); see also a series of articles on *Sensōron* published in *Sensō Sekinin Kenkyū* 27 (spring 2000): 35–57.

54. Bill O'Reilly, *Culture Warrior* (New York: Broadway, 2006); see also Jacob Heilbrunn's review in the *New York Times Book Review*, January 14, 2007.

55. Kobayashi blends well-known photographs of actual events with his own drawing to heighten their impact—or to completely change the story—and Bill O'Reilly launches his attack on "secular-progressive fanatics" by beginning his book with an imagined State of the Union Address in 2020 from the equally fantastical president of the United States, Gloria Hernandez. See O'Reilly, *Culture Warrior*, pp. 9–13.

56. Kobayashi, *Sensōron*, p. 38.

57. Kobayashi, *Sensōron* 2, pp. 9–31.

58. Ibid., p. 280.

59. Ibid., p. 298.

60. Kato Kyoko, "Fuin sareta Shosho Soko o Yomitoku," *Bungei Shunjū* (July 2003): 94–113.

61. Ibid., p. 97.

62. Quoted in ibid., p. 95.

63. The South Korean journalist Koh Sung-il noted that the October 2003 issue of *Bungei Shunju* continues in this vein, leading him to describe a resurgence of support for Hirohito in Japan. See "Muneh Chunju, 'Hirohito Shideh' Chondanghwa Tukchip," Yonhap Wire Service, September 17, 2003. Arguably, this find is of a piece with the discovery of a document that appeared in July 2006 expressing the emperor's apparent misgivings about including war criminals in Japan's Yasukuni Shrine as well as the March 2007 discovery of the diary of the emperor's wartime chamberlain which suggests that the emperor did not want to fight a war with China because he feared Russia.

3. ILLEGAL JAPAN

1. AP Wire Service, June 17, 2000.

2. See Bruce Cumings's enduring analysis in *The Origins of the Korean War: Liberation and the Emergence of Separate Regimes* (Princeton, N.J.: Princeton University Press 1981), esp. chaps. 3 and 4.

3. Cumings, *The Origins of the Korean War*, p. 108.

4. Ibid.

5. Cumings has long stressed that "Stalin permitted joint action in a region where he had the power to take control" (*Origins*, p. 121). See also historian Tsuyoshi Hasegawa's more recent discussion in *Racing the Enemy: Stalin, Truman, and the Surrender of Japan* (Cambridge, Mass.: Harvard University Press, 2005).

6. See Charles Armstrong, *The North Korean Revolution, 1945–1950* (Ithaca, N.Y.: Cornell University Press, 2004).

7. The Korean writer Yi Sang's 1936 story, "Wings," most famously describes Koreans' inability to protest Japanese rule as well as what he viewed as a widespread, resigned collaboration with it. The story ends with the young Korean male protagonist committing suicide by leaping off a Japanese department store in downtown colonized Seoul.

8. Edwin Pauley, *Report on Japanese Reparations to the President of the United States, November 1945 to April 1, 1946* (Washington, D.C.: Government Printing Office, 1948), p. 12. The value of assets in the northern part of the country was higher than the south—again a point that is difficult to conceive today—because the Japanese had targeted their heavy indus-

tries there while maintaining the south in a state of underdevelopment as its "rice basket."

9. Begin with Keith Howard, ed., *True Stories of the Korean Comfort Women* (London: Cassell, 1996).

10. For elaboration, see my book, *Japan's Colonization of Korea: Discourse and Power* (Honolulu: University of Hawaii Press, 2005).

11. Catalogued in Peter Lee, ed., *Sourcebook of Korean Civilization*, 2 vols. (New York: Columbia University Press, 1996), 2:350–351.

12. Ho Wi's demands are also published in Lee, *Sourcebook*, pp. 406–407.

13. The best treatment in English of this issue is Andre Schmid, *Korea between Empires, 1895–1919* (New York: Columbia University Press, 2002).

14. See Second Exhibition Hall on their Web site, which offers a virtual tour in Korean, Japanese, English, and Chinese, http://www.independence.or.kr (accessed June 12, 2006).

15. An excellent resource is the Supreme Commander for Allied Powers, General Headquarters, Statistics and Reports Section, *History of the Non-Military Activities of the Occupation of Japan* (Tokyo: SCAP, 1952).

16. *Chosun Ilbo*, June 8, 1949 (also quoted in Cheong, *The Politics of Anti-Japanese Sentiment in South Korea*, p. 26.).

17. In English, one of the best windows on this moment is Cho Chong-rae's novel, *Playing with Fire*, trans. Chun Kyung-ja, East Asian series (Ithaca, N.Y.: Cornell University Press, 1997).

18. "The Korean Government's Refutation of the Japanese Government's Views Concerning Dokdo ('Takeshima') Dated July 13, 1953," included on Mark S. Lovmo's magnificent Web site, http://www.geocities.com/mlovmo (accessed March 10, 2006).

19. Ironically, today even South Korea's government is nervous about this state of amnesia and is backing a project to construct a "Hall of Democracy" to ensure that the nation's young learn at least an officially approved version of the recent past.

20. *Korea Herald*, January 2007.

21. Presidential Truth Commission on Suspicious Deaths of the Republic of Korea (First Term Report, 10.2000–10.2002), *A Hard Journey to Justice* (Seoul: Samin Books, 2004).

22. Ibid., p. 37.

23. Han Sang-bum, "Head Commissioner's Message," in *Hard Journey to Justice*, p. 17.

24. Sixty-five percent of the "suspicious deaths" the commission investigated occurred under Chun Doo-hwan's regime in the 1980s.

25. Choi In-Hoon, "The Voice of the Governor General," in Chun Kyung-Ja, trans. and comp., *The Voice of the Governor General and Other Stories of Modern Korea* (Norwalk, Conn.: EastBridge, 2002), pp. 165–185.

26. Sarah Soh has quite a number of thoughtful essays as well as an excellent manuscript on the history of the comfort women and the problems in their quest for apology and reparations. Begin with Soh, "Japan's Responsibility Toward Comfort Women Survivors," available online, http://www.icasinc.org/lectures/soh3.html (accessed June 5, 2006).

27. See http://www.vday.org/main.html; http://www.vday.org/contents/vcampaigns/spotlight/comfortwomen (both accessed November 10, 2006).

28. For the testimonies as well as the Web cast that shows the comfort women questioning the congressmen, see http://foreignaffairs.house.gov/hearing_notice.asp?id=763 (accessed February 27, 2007).

29. *New York Times*, March 6, 2007.

30. For a moving history of the Wednesday Demonstration protests in front of the Japanese Embassy in Seoul, which reached its seven hundredth gathering on March 15, 2006, see http://www.womenandwar.net/.

31. The Japanese journalist Senda Kako was one of the pioneering forces, and her 1992 synopsis of her efforts is an excellent account of her own work as well as collaboration with others. See Senda, *Jugun Ianfu to Tennō* (Comfort Women and the Emperor) (Kyoto: Kamogawa Shuppan, 1992).

32. The full text is available at http://www.mofa.go.jp/policy/women/fund/state9308.html.

33. Susan Moeller, *Compassion Fatigue: How the Media Sell Disease, Famine, War, and Death* (New York: Routledge, 1999).

34. The unstructured dialogue of Byun Kyung-joo's monumental documentary trilogy, *The Murmuring* (1995), *Habitual Sadness* (1997), and *My Own Breathing* (1999), drives this powerfully home.

35. Kim Dae-jung and Okamoto Atsushi, "Kokuminteki Koryu to Yuko no Jidai o," (Toward a More Citizen-Oriented Pattern of Exchange) in *Sekai*, no. 653 (1998): 61.

36. The historian William Underwood doggedly chronicles the Chinese forced labor cases, with numerous reports posted to japanofocus.org.

37. The journalist Kinue Tokudome passionately follows this issue regarding American POWs, the only group likely to make any progress with

this law. Among her many articles and books, see "POW Forced Labor Lawsuits Against Japanese Companies," Japan Policy Research Institute Working Paper No. 82, November 2001, and published online at http://www.jpri.org/publications/workingpapers/wp82.html (accessed February 10, 2007).

38. *Hwang Geum Joo et al. v. Japan*, U.S. District Court for the District of Columbia, Case No. 00-CV-2233.

39. *Hwang Geum Joo et al. v. Japan*, United States Court of Appeals for the District of Columbia, Case No. 01-7169.

40. *Che 6-7 Ch'a Han-Il Huitam; Ch'onggugwon Kwanryon Munsuh* (Seoul: Han'guk Ch'ulpanwon, 2005).

4. HISTORY OUT OF BOUNDS

1. See *Donga Ilbo* and the *Korea Herald*, November 28, 2002.

2. The U.S. Embassy in Seoul continues to maintain an explanatory section on its Web site, http://seoul.usembassy.gov/june13acc.html (accessed October 10, 2006).

3. One particularly enterprising South Korean nongovernmental organization (NGO) recorded an excellent DVD in 2002 chronicling South Korea's military involvement in the Vietnam War. In addition to some astonishing footage, the disc contains numerous oral testimonies describing atrocities that Koreans committed against Vietnamese, as well as efforts to promote reconciliation today. See Institute of Democracy and Society/Cyber NGO Resource Center, *Mian haeyo, Pet'tunam: Chonchaeng ui kiok uro ssunun p'yonghwa iyagi, Pet'tunamjon tasibogi* (We're Sorry, Vietnam: Another Look at the Vietnam War, The Story of Peace through Memories of War) (Seoul, 2002), http://www.demos.or.kr.

4. An excellent book is available in Korean and Japanese describing select incidents involving South Korean civilians and U.S. soldiers since 1950. See From Nogunri to Maehyangri Publication Committee, *Nogunri e su Maehyangri kkaji* (Seoul: Kippun Jayu, 2001) (the Japanese translation is published by the Osaka branch of Deep Freedom, 2002).

5. *New York Times*, January 12, 2001; *Washington Post*, January 12, 2001. Also, the Public Broadcasting Service has a highly useful online archive of events, as well as a chronicle of the coverage of No Gun Ri and links to documents, http://www.pbs.org.

6. Less than two months later, on January 26, 2003, a U.S. Air Force spy plane flying a reconnaissance mission crashed into the town of Hwasung twenty miles south of Seoul. No one died, and yet Brigadier General Mark G. Beesley, vice commander of the Seventh Air Force, immediately visited the four mildly injured civilians, because, as journalist Don Kirk explained, the "U.S. military command [is] wary of providing more ammunition for foes of American troop presence [in South Korea], [and Beesley] promptly expressed sorrow for the accident" (*New York Times*, January 27, 2003).

7. For coverage of the event and the history of the developing story, see Charles Hanley, Sang-hun Choe, and Martha Mendoza, *The Bridge at No Gun Ri: A Hidden Nightmare of the Korean War* (New York: Henry Holt, 2001).

8. William Cohen to Louis Caldera, September 30, 1999, catalogued as Enclosure 1, in Chapter 1, United States Army, *Report of the No Gun Ri Review* (January 2001). The *Report* is available in its entirety at http://www.army.mil/nogunri/ (accessed October 1, 2006).

9. William Cohen to Louis Caldera, October 15, 1999, Enclosure 2, Chapter 1, in *Report*.

10. Review members are listed in Enclosure 5, Chapter 1, in *Report*.

11. Chapter 5, Section 8, in *Report*.

12. Chapter 5, Section 5, in *Report*,

13. AP Wire Service, January 13, 2001.

14. Bill Clinton, January 11, 2001 on *PBS NewsHour* Web site: http://www.pbs.org/newshour/media/nogunri/index.html (accessed October 15, 2006).

15. *Korea Times*, September 27, 2006.

16. Chapter 2, Section 2, in *Report*.

17. See Sahr Conway-Lanz, *Collateral Damage: Americans, Noncombatant Immunity, and Atrocity after World War II* (New York: Routledge, 2006).

18. See Kai Bird and Lawrence Lifschultz, eds., *Hiroshima's Shadows: Writings on the Denial of History and the Smithsonian Controversy* (New York: Pamphleteer's Press, 1998); see also Robert Jay Lifton and Greg Mitchell, *Hiroshima in America: A Half Century of Denial* (New York: Harper Perennial, 1996).

19. In English, begin with Thomas Havens, *Valley of Darkness: Japanese People and World War II* (New York: Norton, 1978).

20. Wilfred Burchett, *Shadows of Hiroshima* (London: Verso, 1983), p. 25.

21. "The Atomic Plague," *Daily Express*, September 5, 1945, p. 1; see Paul Boyer, *By the Bombs Early Light: American Thought and Culture at the Dawn of the*

Atomic Age (New York: Pantheon, 1985); see also Beverley Deepe Keever, *News Zero* (Monroe, Maine.: Common Courage Press, 2004).

22. The September 4 evening editions of some American newspapers such as the *Boston Globe* carried stories, including the account of the sick by the United Press correspondent James McGlincy. Yet, as a matter of record, and because of all sorts of imperial legacies such as time zones, the London paper counts as the "first."

23. "The Atomic Plague," *Daily Express*, September 5, 1945. See also Burchett, *Shadows*, p. 34.

24. Mark Selden, "Nagasaki 1945: While Independents Were Scorned, Embed Won Pulitzer," August 2005, http://www.japanfocus.org/prod ucts/details/1616.

25. Burchett, *Shadows*, p. 30

26. Ibid., p. 35.

27. *New York Times*, September 5, 1945, "Visit to Hiroshima Proves It World's Most Damaged City," p. 1. See also McGlincy's continued coverage in the *Boston Globe*.

28. The journalist Amy Goodman has drawn attention to this moment in her online essay published with David Goodman, August 10, 2004 "Hiroshima Cover-up: How the War Department's Timesman Won a Pulitzer," http://www.commondreams.org/views04/0810-01.htm.

29. Burchett, *Shadows*, p. 41.

30. *New York Times*, September 5, 1945.

31. Keever, *News Zero*, p. 78

32. Goodman, "Hiroshima Cover-up."

33. Keever, *News Zero*, p. 78.

34. *New York Times*, September 12, 1945.

35. Historian Barton J. Bernstein's brief discussion of the numbers game involved in projecting American casualty figures should be required reading for all. See Bernstein, "A Post-War Myth: 500,000 U.S. Lives Saved," in Bird and Lifschultz, *Hiroshima's Shadows*, pp. 130–134. Bernstein has even located one document in army archives from July 1945 that places the estimate as low as 20,000.

36. John Hersey, *Hiroshima* (New York: Knopf, 1946).

37. See James Hershberg, *James B. Conant: Harvard to Hiroshima and the Making of the Nuclear Age* (Stanford: Stanford University Press, 1995).

38. See Barton Bernstein, "Seizing the Contested Terrain of Early Nuclear History," in Bird and Lifschultz, *Hiroshima's Shadows*, pp. 163–196.

39. Conant to Bundy (September 23, 1946), Conant Presidential Papers, quoted in Barton J. Bernstein, "Seizing the Contested Terrain of Early Nuclear History," in Kay Bird and Lawrence Lifschultz, eds., *Hiroshima's Shadows: Writings on the Denial of History and the Smithsonian Controversy* (Stony Creek, Conn.: The Pamphleteer's Press, 1998), p. 166.

40. See Kai Bird and Martin Sherwin, *American Prometheus: The Triumph and Tragedy of J. Robert Oppenheimer* (New York: Vintage, 2006), chaps. 22, 23.

41. Reprinted in Bird and Lifschultz, *Shadows*, pp. 197–210.

42. Quoted in Alfred Steinberg, *The Man from Missouri: The Life and Times of Harry S. Truman* (New York: Putnam's, 1962), p. 259.

43. Kobayashi Masaki, *Tokyo Saiban* (International Military Tribunal for the Far East) (1983) (Released on DVD, Tokyo: Kodansha, 2000), Disc 1; T1: 47 (1:12–1:18).

44. In Bird and Sherwin, *American Prometheus*, pp. 438–453.

45. Holly Barker, *Bravo for the Marshallese: Regaining Control in a Post-Nuclear, Post-Colonial World* (Belmont, Calif.: Wadsworth/Thomson Learning, 2004), p. xiii.

46. Robert Stone, *Radio Bikini: The Most Terrifying and Unbelievable Story of the Nuclear Age* (Released on DVD by New Video Group, 2003).

47. Donald F. McHenry, *Micronesia: Trust Betrayed* (Washington, D.C.: Carnegie Endowment for International Peace, 1975); see also Jane Dibblin, *Day of Two Suns: U.S. Nuclear Testing and the Pacific Islanders* (New York: New Amsterdam Books, 1990).

48. The "tuna panic," as it was known temporarily, devastated Japan's fishing industry. Prices plummeted as Japanese stopped eating fish entirely, and fishermen across the country were impoverished overnight.

49. See http://www.atomicbombmuseum.org (accessed October 20, 2006). See also George Totten and Tamio Kawakami, "Gensuikyo and the Peace Movement in Japan," *Asian Survey* 4 (May 1964): 833–841.

50. For the significance of such women-driven political momentum, see Robin LeBlanc, *Bicycle Citizens: The Political World of the Japanese Housewife* (Berkeley: University of California Press, 1999).

51. Letter from John M. Allison to Shigemitsu Mamoru, January 4, 1955, Tokyo, collected at the Archives of the Foreign Ministry, Tokyo, Japan (reel A-1 01–419).

52. Hirano Keiji, *Chugoku Shimbun Peace News*, Kyodo Wire Service, February 29, 2004.

53. AP Wire Service, April 15, 1995.

54. On May 16, 1997, Clinton apologized to five of the eight remaining survivors of a forty-eight-year-long study that withheld treatment; during his March 1998 trip to Uganda, Clinton made the now famous speech, which, as Alfred Brophy argued subsequently, necessitated President George W. Bush's visit during his first term; on March 10, 1999, Clinton addressed the issue of the death squads and the massacres of Mayans. See Alfred Brophy, *Reparations: Pro and Con* (New York: Oxford University Press, 2006).

55. The International Red Cross has a succinct and informative Web site: http://www.icrc.org/web/eng/siteeng0.nsf/html/5KSK7Q (accessed May 1, 2007).

BIBLIOGRAPHY

ARCHIVES, GOVERNMENT REPORTS, OFFICIAL PUBLICATIONS

Gatz, Karen L., ed. *Foreign Relations of the United States, 1964–1968.* Vol. 29, pt. 1, *Korea.* Washington, D.C.: U.S. Government Printing Office, 2000.

Horace Capron Papers, Yale University.

Ito Hirobumi. *Commentaries on the Constitution of The Empire of Japan* (1889). Translated by Ito Miyoji. Tokyo: Chuo University Press, 1906.

Pauley, Edwin. *Report on Japanese Reparations to the President of the United States, November 1945 to April 1, 1946.* Washington, D.C.: Government Printing Office, 1948.

Presidential Truth Commission on Suspicious Deaths of the Republic of Korea. First Term Report, 10.2000–10.2002. *A Hard Journey to Justice.* Seoul: Samin Books, 2004.

Supreme Commander for Allied Powers, General Headquarters, Statistics and Reports Section. *History of the Non-Military Activities of the Occupation of Japan.* Tokyo: SCAP, 1952.

United Nations, Treaty Series. *Treaties and International Agreements Registered or Filed and Recorded with the Secretariat of the United Nations.* Vol. 583. New York: United Nations Publications, 1966.

United States Army. *Report of the No Gun Ri Review.* January 2001.

United States Department of State, Foreign Relations of the United States, 1945. Vol. 8, *The Far East.* Washington, D.C.: State Department/GPO, 1971.

United States Department of State, Record Group 59, General Records of the Department of State. *Records of the U.S. Department of State Relating to the Internal Affairs of Japan, 1945–1954.* Washington, D.C., Diplomatic Branch, National Archives.

WEB SITES AND WEB ARTICLES

http://www.army.mil/nogunri/
http://www.asahi.com/column/funabashi/eng
http://www.atomicbombmuseum.org
http://www.commondreams.org
http://www.demos.or.kr
http://www.dokdo.go.kr
http://www.dokdomuseum.go.kr
http://english.president.go.kr
http://foreignaffairs.house.gov/hearing_notice.asp?id=763
http://www.geocities.com/mlovmo
http://www.icasinc.org/lectures/soh3.html
http://www.icrc.org/web/eng/siteeng0.nsf/html/5KSK7Q
http://www.independence.or.kr
http://www.isop.ucla.edu/eas/documents/peace1951.htm
http://www.japanfocus.org
http://www.jpri.org/publications/workingpapers/wp82.html
http://www.kaijipr.or.jp
http://www.kocean.org
http://www.mofa.go.jp/policy/maritime/japan/index.html
http://www.mofa.go.jp/policy/women/fund/state9308.html
http://www.mofa.go.jp/region/asia-paci/takeshima/position.html
http://www.mofat.go.kr/index.html
http://www.mofat.go.kr/pdffiles/Eastsea1.pdf
http://parks.seoul.go.kr/main/english/independence/prison.htm
http://www.pbs.org
http://seoul.usembassy.gov/june13acc.html
http://www.umimori.jp
http://uniorb.com/ATREND/Japanwatch/wsdramafever.htm
http://www.vday.org/main.html
http://www.vday.org/contents/vcampaigns/spotlight/comfortwomen
http://www.womenandwar.net/

NEWSPAPERS

Asahi Shimbun
Boston Globe

Chosun Ilbo
Donga Ilbo
Hankyoreh
Japan Times
Korea Herald
Kyunghyang Shinmun
Mainichi Shimbun
New York Times
Sankei Shimbun
Segye Ilbo
Washington Post

BOOKS AND JOURNALS

Amino Yoshihiko. *Iwanami Kōza Nihon Tsushi*, Vol. 1, *Nihon Rettō to Jinrui Shakai* (The Japanese Archipelago and Its People and Society). Tokyo: Iwanami Shoten, 1993.

Arai Shinichi and Iko Toshiya. "Compendium List of Aplogies." *Sekai* (World), no. 696 (December 2001): 178–196.

Armstrong, Charles. *The North Korean Revolution, 1945–1950*. Ithaca, N.Y.: Cornell University Press, 2004.

Barker, Holly. *Bravo for the Marshallese: Regaining Control in a Post-Nuclear, Post-Colonial World*. Belmont, Calif.: Wadsworth/Thomson Learning, 2004.

Bird, Kai, and Lawrence Lifschultz, eds. *Hiroshima's Shadows: Writings on the Denial of History and the Smithsonian Controversy*. New York: Pamphleteer's Press, 1998.

Bird, Kai, and Martin Sherwin. *American Prometheus: The Triumph and Tragedy of J. Robert Oppenheimer*. New York: Vintage, 2006.

Bix, Herbert. *Hirohito and the Making of Modern Japan*. New York: Harper's, 2001.

Boyer, Paul. *By the Bombs Early Light: American Thought and Culture at the Dawn of the Atomic Age*. New York: Pantheon, 1985.

Brophy, Alfred. *Reparations: Pro and Con*. New York: Oxford University Press, 2006.

Burchett, Wilfred. *Shadows of Hiroshima*. London: Verso, 1983.

Cha, Victor. D. *Alignment Despite Antagonism: The United States–Korea–Japan Security Triangle*. Stanford: Stanford University Press, 1999.

Cheong Sung-hwa, *The Politics of Anti-Japanese Sentiment in Korea: Japanese–South Korean Relations under the American Occupation, 1945–1952*. Westport, Conn.: Greenwood, 1991.

Chi Myon Gwan, and Igarashi Masahiro, eds. *Nikkan no Sogo Rikai to Sengo Hosho* (New Japan-Korea Partnership and Postwar Compensation). Tokyo: Nihon Hyoronsha, 2002.

Cho Chong-rae. *Playing with Fire*. Translated by Chun Kyung-ja. East Asian Publication Series. Ithaca, N.Y.: Cornell University Press, 1997.

Choi Chungmoo, ed. "The Comfort Women: Colonialism, War, and Sex." Special issue, *Positions: East Asia Cultures Critique* 5, no. 1 (Spring 1997).

Choi In-Hoon. "The Voice of the Governor General." In Chun Kyung-Ja, ed., *The Voice of the Governor General and Other Stories of Modern Korea*. Norwalk, Conn.: EastBridge, 2002.

Clifford, Rebecca. "Cleansing History, Cleansing Japan: Kobayashi Yoshinori's Analects of War and Japan's Revisionist Revival." Oxford University, Nissan Occasional Papers Series, 2004.

Conway-Lanz, Sahr. *Collateral Damage: Americans, Noncombatant Immunity, and Atrocity after World War II*. New York: Routledge, 2006.

Cumings, Bruce. *The Origins of the Korean War: Liberation and the Emergence of Separate Regimes*. Princeton, N.J.: Princeton University Press, 1981.

Dibblin, Jane. *Day of Two Suns: U.S. Nuclear Testing and the Pacific Islanders*. New York: New Amsterdam Books, 1990.

Dower, John. *Embracing Defeat: Japan in the Wake of World War II*. New York: Norton, 1999.

Dudden, Alexis. *Japan's Colonization of Korea: Discourse and Power*. Honolulu: University of Hawai'i Press, 2005.

Fujitani, Takashi, Geoffrey M. White, and Lisa Yoneyama, eds. *Perilous Memories: The Asia-Pacific War(s)*. Durham: Duke University Press, 2001.

Funabashi Yoichi. "Kako Kokufuku Seisaku o Teisho Suru" (A Proposal for a Policy to Overcome the Past). *Sekai*, no. 692 (2001): 48–62.

Hanley, Charles, Sang-hun Choe, and Martha Mendoza. *The Bridge at No Gun Ri: A Hidden Nightmare of the Korean War*. New York: Henry Holt, 2001.

Harootunian, Harry. "Japan's Long Postwar: The Trick of Memory and the Ruse of History." *South Atlantic Quarterly* 99, no. 4 (Fall 2000): 715–739.

Hasegawa, Tsuyoshi. *Racing the Enemy: Stalin, Truman, and the Surrender of Japan*. Cambridge, Mass.: Harvard University Press, 2005.

Havens, Thomas. *Valley of Darkness: Japanese People and World War II.* New York: Norton, 1978.

Hersey, John. *Hiroshima.* New York: Knopf, 1946.

Hershberg, James. *James B. Conant: Harvard to Hiroshima and the Making of the Nuclear Age.* Stanford: Stanford University Press, 1995.

Howard, Keith, ed. *True Stories of the Korean Comfort Women.* London: Cassell, 1996.

Iwabuchi, Koichi. "Return to Asia," "Nostalgia for a (Different) Asian Modernity: Media Consumption of 'Asia' in Japan." *Positions: East Asia Cultures Critique* 10, no. 3 (Winter 2002): 547–573.

Jenkins, Charles. *Kokuhaku* (To Tell The Truth). Tokyo: Kadokawa Shoten, 2005.

Johnston, William. "From Feudal Fishing Villages to an Archipelago's People: The Historiographical Journey of Amino Yoshihiko." Harvard University, Reischauer Institute Occasional Papers in Japanese Studies, March 2005.

Kajimura Hideki. "The Question of Takeshima/Tokdo." *Chōsen Kenkyū,* no. 182 (September 1978); reprinted in *Korea Observer* 28, no. 3 (Autumn 1997).

Kato Kyoko. "Fuin sareta Shosho Soko o Yomitoku." *Bungei Shunju* (2003): 94–113.

Keever, Beverley Deepe. *News Zero.* Monroe, Me.: Common Courage Press, 2004.

Kim Dae-jung and Okamoto Atsushi. "Kokuminteki Koryu to Yuko no Jidai o." (Toward a More Citizen-Oriented Pattern of Exchange). *Sekai,* no. 653 (1998).

Kim Young Koo. *A Pursuit of Truth in the Dokdo Island Issue: Letters to a Young Japanese Man.* Seoul: Bub Young Sa, 2003.

Kobayashi Yoshinori. *Sensōron* (On War). Tokyo: Gentosha, 1998.

———. *Sensōron* 2 (On War 2). Tokyo: Gentosha, 2001.

LeBlanc, Robin. *Bicycle Citizens: The Political World of the Japanese Housewife.* Berkeley: University of California Press, 1999.

Lee, Peter, ed. *Sourcebook of Korean Civilization.* New York: Columbia University Press, 1996.

Lifton, Robert Jay, and Greg Mitchell. *Hiroshima in America: A Half Century of Denial.* New York: Harper Perennial, 1996.

McHenry, Donald. *Micronesia: Trust Betrayed.* Washington, D.C.: Carnegie Endowment for International Peace, 1975.

McNeill, David. "Selective Pain: Kidnapping, Contemporary Japan, and Media Obsession," *Japan Focus*, August 2006. Available at http://www.japanfocus.org/products/details/2231

Maeda Tamon. "Ningen sengen no uchi-soto" (The Inside Story of the Emperor's Declaration). *Bungei Shunjû*, March 1962.

Moeller, Robert G. "On the History of Man-made Destruction: Loss, Death, Memory, and Germany in the Bombing War." *History Workshop Journal*, no. 61 (Fall 2006): 103–134.

Moeller, Susan. *Compassion Fatigue: How the Media Sell Disease, Famine, War, and Death*. New York: Routledge, 1999.

Morris-Suzuki, Tessa. *The Past Within Us: Media, Memory, History*. New York: Verso, 2005.

——. "When Is a Terrorist Not a Terrorist?" *Japan Focus*, October 2003. Available at http://www.japanfocus.org/products/details/1838

Nogunri to Maehyangri Publication Committee. *Nogunri e suh Maehyangri kkaji* (From Nogunri to Maehyangri). Seoul: Kippun Jayu, 2001.

Olick, Jeffrey. "Genre Memories and Memory Genres: A Dialogical Analysis of May 8, 1945, Commemorations in the Federal Republic of Germany." *American Sociological Review* 64 (1999): 381–402.

O'Reilly, Bill. *Culture Warrior*. New York: Broadway, 2006.

Postone, Moishe, and Eric Santner, eds. *Catastrophe and Meaning: The Holocaust and the Twentieth Century*. Chicago: University of Chicago Press, 2003.

Schmid, Andre. *Korea Between Empires, 1895–1919*. New York: Columbia University Press, 2002.

Sebald, W. G. *On the Natural History of Destruction*. New York: Penguin, 2004.

Selden, Mark. "Nagasaki 1945: While Independents Were Scorned, Embed Won Pulitzer." *Japan Focus*, August 2005. Available at http://www.japanfocus.org/products/details/1616

Senda Kako. *Jugun Ianfu to Tennō* (Comfort Women and the Emperor). Kyoto: Kamogawa Shuppan, 1992.

Shimizu, Sayuri. *Creating a People of Plenty: The United States and Japan's Economic Alternatives, 1950–1960*. Kent, Ohio: Kent State University Press, 2001.

Shin, Gi-Wook, and Michael Robinson, eds. *Colonial Modernity in Korea*. Cambridge, Mass.: Harvard University Press, 1999.

Steinberg, Alfred. *The Man from Missouri: The Life and Times of Harry S. Truman*. New York: Putnam's, 1962.

Tokudome, Kinue. "POW Forced Labor Lawsuits against Japanese Companies." Japan Policy Research Institute Working Paper No. 82. November 2001. Available at http://www.jpri.org/publications/workingpapers/wp82.html

Totten, George, and Tamio Kawakami. "Gensuikyo and the Peace Movement in Japan." *Asian Survey* 4 (May 1964): 833–841.

Treat, John. *Writing Ground Zero: Japanese Literature and the Atomic Bomb*. Chicago: University of Chicago Press, 1996.

Umeno Masanobu, and Sawada Tatsu, eds. *Sensōron/Mosoron* (On War/On Hate). Tokyo: Kyoiku Shiryo Shuppankai, 1999.

Underwood, William. "Names, Bones and Unpaid Wages: Reparations for Korean Forced Labor in Japan." Parts 1 and 2. *Japan Focus* (September 2006). Available at http://www.japanfocus.org/products/details/2219

Yamano Sharin. *Manga Kenkanryū* (Hating the Korean Wave). Tokyo: Shinyusha, 2005.

FILMS

Byun Kyung-joo, *The Murmuring*. Seoul, 1995.

———. *Habitual Sadness*. Seoul, 1997.

———. *My Own Breathing*. Seoul, 1999.

Cyber NGO Resource Center. *Mian haeyo, Pet'tunam: Chŏnchaeng ŭi kiŏk uro ssunun p'yŏnghwa iyagi, Pet'tunamjŏn tasibogi* (We're Sorry, Vietnam: Another Look at the Vietnam War, The Story of Peace through Memories of War). Seoul, 2002.

Kim Hyeon-Seok. *YMCA Baseball Team*. Seoul, 2002.

Kobayashi Masaki. *Tokyo Saiban* (International Military Tribunal for the Far East). Tokyo, 1983.

Matsui Minoru. *Riben Guizi* (Japanese Devils). Tokyo, 2001.

Oguri Kohei. *Kayako no tame ni* (For Kayako). Tokyo, 1984.

Stone, Robert. *Radio Bikini: The Most Terrifying and Unbelievable Story of the Nuclear Age*. New York, 1988.

Tong, Nancy. *In the Name of the Emperor*. New York, 1996.

INDEX

Kato Kyoko, 61
kidnapping, 49–56
Kim Dae-jung, 45, 47, 84, 91–92,
    100–101
Kim Hak-soon, 89
Kim Hyeon-seok, 76
Kim Il Sung, 69, 71, 75
Kim Jong-il, 50–51, 56, 71–72, 94
Kim Young-sam, 84
Kishi Nobusuke, 85
Kissinger, Henry, 122
Kobayashi Yoshinori, 57–61,
    143n143
Koizumi Junichiro, 3–4, 6, 46, 50,
    143n49
Kono Yohei, 89–90
Korea: ancient dynastic maps, 23;
    anti-Japanese riots (1919), 9, 72;
    demilitarized zone (DMZ), 66;
    governments-in-exile, 75; Japanese
    colonization of, 6–7, 19, 42, 72–74;
    Japanese past as "colonial," 70–71;
    MacArthur Line, 80–82;
    North-South relations, 42–43;
    position papers, 82–83; Righteous
    Army (Uibyong) insurgency, 74–76;
    self-government attempts, 68–70.
    See also North Korea; South Korea
Korean Council, 93
"Korean Government's Refutation of
    the Japanese Government's Views
    Concerning Dokdo," 82
Koreans in Japan, 7–9, 53–54
Korean War (1950–53), 23–24, 66,
    82
Korean Wave, 47–49
Korean Women's Council for Women
    Drafted into Sexual Slavery, 89
Kuboyama Aikichi, 123, 125

Kurile/Chishima islands, 13
Kyushu island, 80

Laurence, William "Atomic Bill," 112,
    113–116
Lawrence, William H., 112–113
lawsuits, comfort women and, 92–93
Lee Hoi-chang, 99
Lucky Dragon incident, 124, 126–127

MacArthur, Douglas, 37, 69, 80, 108,
    109
MacArthur Line, 80–82
MacDonald, Gabriella Kirk, 93
Manchurian Army (Japan), 10
Manhattan Project, 113, 117
Marine Day, 12–16
"Maritime Watch" group (Umimori),
    14
Marshall Islands, 120–122
McCarthyism, 120
McCullough, David, 118–119
"Military First!" policy (North Korea),
    72
military occupation, as term, 65
Ministry of Foreign Affairs and Trade
    (South Korea), 17–18
Ministry of Foreign Affairs (Japan),
    17
"Minor Islands Adjacent to Japan
    Proper: Minor Islands in the Sea of
    Japan" (Japan, 1946), 21–22
Min Yonghwan, 77
Miyazawa Kiichi, 60, 89
Morris-Suzuki, Tessa, 16
multinational companies, 13
Murayama Tomoichi, 40–41, 45
Museum of Natural History (New
    York City), 8

Nagasaki, bombing of, 66, 107–108, 114–115
Nakayama Nariaki, 39
Nanjing Massacre, 39
National Security Law (1948, Korea), 83–84, 86
neo-colonies, 68
New York Times, 112–114
Nippon Foundation, 14, 15
no-go zones, 121–122
No Gun Ri incident, 101–106
North Korea (Democratic People's Republic of Korea): abduction issue, 49–56; as "axis of evil," 26, 127; brought into being, 70; as Joseon, 24; lack of acknowledgment, 45–46; naming of sea and, 28–29; nuclear weapons program, 49–51, 106; People's Army, 71–72
nuclear weapons, 107–108; bombing of Hiroshima and Nagasaki, 66, 107–119; *Bravo* test, 122, 125–127, 150n48; Japanese opposition to, 124–125; in Marshall Islands, 120–122; North Korean program, 49–51, 106; "saved lives" rhetoric, 114, 117–118, 128; U.S. determination to keep, 128–129

Obuchi Keizo, 45, 47
official documents, 16–19
Okazaki Tomoko, 140n24
Okinawa, 20–21, 22
Olick, Jeffrey, 39
"Operation Crossroads," 121
Oppenheimer, J. Robert, 120
O'Reilly, Bill, 58, 143n143

"Overrun Nations" postage stamp series, 67–68
Ozawa Ichiro, 132

Pak Poe, 8
Park Chung-hee, 10, 44, 85–86, 94
Park Geun-hye, 85
Peace Line. *See* Rhee Line
People's Army (North Korea), 71–72
Philippines, 67, 68
popular culture, 47–49, 142n41
Portsmouth Peace Treaty Conference, 8
postage stamps: South Korean, 82–83; U.S. "Overrun Nations" stamp series, 67–68
present, past used to manipulate, 5–6, 24, 45–46
Provisional Government of the Korean Republic, 74
public education, 35, 38–40, 63

Rabinowitch, Eugene, 117
Radio Bikini (film), 121
Reischauer, Edwin O., 43–45
resource issue, 78–81
Rhee, Syngman, 69–70, 75, 81, 82
Rhee Line, 82, 86
Rice, Condoleezza, 25, 26
Righteous Army (*Uibyong*) insurgency, 74–76
right-wing extremist groups (Japan), 14–15, 56, 57–61, 127
Roh Moo-hyun, 4, 26, 30, 63–64, 99, 140n24
Roosevelt, Franklin D., 66–68
Roosevelt, Theodore, 8
ruse of history, 5–6, 46, 77–78
Rusk, Dean, 43–44, 66

Russia, 13
Russo-Japan War, 8, 68

Sakhalin Island, 86
Samsung corporation, 29
San Francisco Treaty (1951), 20–26,
74, 82, 94; no mention of islands,
21–23
Sasakawa Ryoichi ("Shadowman"), 14
Sato Eisaku, 44
SCAPIN 677 (United States), 21
SCAPIN 1033 (United States), 80
Sebald, W. G., 35
Sebald, William J., 22, 25–26,
137–138n27
Selden, Mark, 109
Sensōron (On War) (Kobayashi), 57–61
Sensōron 2 (On War 2) (Kobayashi), 57
September 11, 2001 attacks, 59
Shadow of Hiroshima (Burchett),
108–113
Shigemetsu Mamoru, 126, 127
Shiina Etsusaburo, 44, 45
Shimane prefecture (Japan), 2–3, 19
Showa Day, 12
Socialists (Japan), 44
Soedaemun jail (Seoul), 9–10
Song Gang-ho, 76
South Korea (Republic of Korea):
communist insurgencies, 82; as
democracy, 84–85; elections, 84,
98–100; human rights inquiries,
84–86; legality of, 83–95; living
conditions, 81–82; military regimes,
83–86; National Security Law,
83–84, 86; normalization with
Japan, 86–87; popular Japanese
culture, 47–49, 142n41; U.S.-backed
dictatorship, 10–11; U.S. occupation

of, 23–26, 65, 67–72; violent
incidents, U.S. military and,
101–106
South Korean Truth Commission,
85–86
"Statement of Mutual Understanding
between the United States and the
Republic of Korea on the No Gun
Ri Investigations," 101–106
Stimson, Henry, 116–117
Stone, Robert, 121
Suginami Appeal, 126
suicide, portrayal of, 77
Szilard, Leo, 117

Tajima Michiji, 61–62
Takano Toshiyuki, 3
Takeshima Day, 2–3
third country, 54–55
Thomson, James C., 44
thought police (kempeitai), 108
Tojo Hideki, 85
Treaty on Basic Relations (1965), 6,
10–11, 43, 86–87; terms of
agreement, 94–95
Truman, Harry, 116, 118, 119–120
Truman (McCullough), 118–119
trusteeship scheme, 68
Tsushima island, 80

Ulleungdo island, 22, 23, 26–30
United States: civilian casualties and,
106–109; congressional hearings on
comfort women, 88–89, 132;
demands for apologies from, 96,
97–100; denial of empire, 67–68;
empire in Korea, 67–72; island
controversy and, 4–5, 22, 24–26;
Japan, occupation of, 20–23; June

2002 tragedy (girls' deaths), 97–98, 107; Korea, occupation of, 10–11, 23–26, 65, 67–72; Korea, violent incidents in, 101–106; North Korea-South Korea relations and, 42–43; War on Terror, 127

U.S. Air Force, bombing incidents, 80, 82, 140–141n25

USS *Missouri*, 109–110

V-Day movement, 88

Vietnam War, 100, 102

Violence Against Women in War-Network Japan, 93

"Voice of the Governor-General, The" (Choi In-hoon), 86–87

Warfield, A.G., 31–32

War on Terror (United States), 127

waters as borders, 15–16; MacArthur Line, 80–81

Weizsäcker, Richard von, 32

"Wings" (Yi), 144n7

Winter Sonata (TV show), 47–49, 55–56

Women's International War Crimes Tribunal on Japan's Military Sexual Slavery, 93

World Conference against Atomic and Hydrogen Bombs, 126

World Cup (2002), 47, 48

Yasukuni Shrine (Tokyo), 5, 7, 8, 91

Year of Friendship, 4

Yi Sang, 144n7

YMCA Baseball Team, (film), 76–77

"Yon-sama" craze, 47–49, 142n41

Yoshida Shigeru, 126

Yu Kwan-soon, 9

zainichi (resident foreigner), 7–8

Important terms / glossary
- Remorse
= Compassion
= posture

SHOW get audio of comfort women!
___ read up: Compassion fatigue
        susan moeller PS 90

PG 95 - find song

VOCAB - good words
___ maelstrom
     palpable